Hurry Up! Join the fastest growing faith based social, business, e-commerce and educational Networking Portal in the world today. How would you like to create real wealth $$$$ doing the same things you're doing on…Facebook, Twitter, LinkedIN and MySpace for FREE!

For Video Tutorials about this Amazing Kingdom Portal:

visit www.mykmcmedia.com.

To SIGN UP and launch your own social networking business:

visit www.mykmcportal.com.

Join hundreds of Kingdom Citizens who have already signed up for this God given portal of blessing.

ENDORSEMENTS

"Have you ever picked up a book and instinctively knew that the power of its revelation could change the hearts of men? That is precisely what I felt when I read *The Spirit of Divine Interception* written by Dr. Francis Myles. As the author eloquently explained the process of interception, I was reminded of event after event when God chose to break into my life to change its outcome. I remember a time many years ago when I was a young Christian. My wife and I were invited to minister in a small sleepy town in East Texas along with a married couple who were our dear friends. At the invitation, my wife felt strongly that we should *not* attend this meeting and at her insistence we decided not to go. The day arrived for the ministry trip, and we spoke briefly with our friends before their lengthy travel to the church. Approximately a half hour later, the couple and their children were involved in a fatal head on collision and three were killed. Friend, we experienced God's Divine interception that day and learned firsthand a valuable lesson. Whether you need insight concerning business, ministry, or family this book will release an understanding of God's ways and His interaction with mankind. In essence, we must allow the Lord to take us to a safe place before the enemy has an opportunity to take us out. I highly recommend that you read this book and gift it to others; it is a must read!" - Apostle Vance D. Russell, Founder of Arise Ministries International, Author of *Victory at the Gates,* www.ariseministries.com

....

"If you don't get anything else out of this book than the understanding of the difference between two similar sounding words: interception (prevention of pain) and intervention (pain followed by a bail out), you will have your whole worldview clarified. As someone who constantly teaches that 'Definitions determine outcomes,' and 'You cannot think past your vocabulary,' I understand the magnitude that the kind of distinctions Dr. Myles makes clear in this book can have on your daily life. If you want to break the cycle of living in trauma and then waiting for God to deliver you, and instead move into a life of quiet victory and peace, then this book is worth your time and effort to understand. Dr. Myles has done the hard work for you. All you have to do is receive." - Dr. Marlene McMillan, www.KingdomLiberty.com.

....

"When Dr. Francis Myles came to my weekly Marketplace Bible Study, he spoke on the difference between 'Divine Interception' and 'Divine Intervention,' to say that I was deeply affected is an understatement. The Lord really spoke to me and reminded me that I had lost thousands of dollars in bad business deals because I refused to obey the technology of divine interception. Through his goodness God 'Intervened' to deliver me from the painful consequences of having ignored the spirit of divine interception. Listening to Dr. Myles that afternoon helped me to connect the dots in my mind. I realized that 'Divine Intervention' is not God's best plan of protection for His Children, 'Interception is.' I highly recommend this incredible book." - John Reaves, Owner of Smokey John's Barbecue Restaurant, Dallas, Texas

....

"When I reflect on my life I now see the times that the Holy Spirit used people and circumstances to try and 'intercept me' on my path to destruction. I didn't listen and destroyed many people who I love dearly. I have paid and am paying the price for my decisions. Praise God however He tells us to forget those things of the past and look at what He is about to do!! Listening to you today made it so clear what my ministry and service to God is…interception. I thought it was intervention but God showed me otherwise today. I am currently working with several Celebrate Recovery groups...I am staying with those groups but as of today my message is changing, from intervention to interception. I want to reach out to men and women who haven't quite reached the bottom yet...there is still time for an interception to take place. Dr. Myles, God bless you and thank you for your profound impact on my life today!" - Wade Raper, Dallas, Texas

....

"Dr. Myles has done it again in this new book on the Spirit of Interception following his latest endeavor on the Order of Melchezidek.

As a business owner and entrepreneur, in both the fuel commodities industry and the media entertainment business in Hollywood, I find it quite common to encounter 'interrupting' entities that consistently engage in practices to hinder or completely stop the flow of business deals. For years, as a believer, I struggled with the 'spiritual' warfare I felt, in dealing with, what I now know to be both national and international principalities, dominating these industries. Not until I came under the influence and anointing of the Order of Melchezidek, did I really fully begin to understand the power of the spirit of interception, to stop these demonic strategies. Just like Abraham of the Old Testament, having the spirit of interception come to him through Melchezidek, the king of Salem, (and what I believe to be an Old Testament visitation of Jesus), when the king of Sodom came to him, (as a prototype of Satan) to steal, kill and destroy his destiny, so have I, personally experienced the angelic dimension and the presence of the 'King of Kings' intercepting the demonic strategies, and wrong business relationships, that could have produced a 'counterfeit' destiny for my life, by operating under this Order of Melchezidek, the highest order in the universe, and the order that Jesus himself operates under in the heavenlies. This book will change the way you think about the marketplace and will give you 'spiritual strategies' to finish well and complete what God has started in you by eliminating frustration and producing supernatural joy in your heart!" - Danny W. Seay, President, SR Energy, LLC; VisionWorks, LLC

....

"Without a doubt this is one of the most awaited and needed messages that will change our understanding of how our great God wants to work in our lives versus how he has had to work in our lives! Every true believer will want to feast from this 'now' word immediately. This will be the message of this decade that will be preached and proclaimed across every denominational line and to think, you get to be one of the first to read it! I promise you that you will never be the same again after reading this powerful, life changing message from my friend Dr. Myles." - Dr. Stan Harris aka Dr. Break Through, 10th degree Black belt, International Speaker, Evangelist, and Best Selling Author, www.DrBreakThrough.com

"The principle of interception must be understood and practiced by every believer in order to live a life of blessing and covenant protection in God. I highly recommend this powerful book by Dr. Francis Myles."
- Myron Golden, CEO, Skillionaire Inc., Author of *Ebony Treasure Map*, www.myrongolden.com

....

"As a prayer leader in the prayer movement one of the greatest challenges that I have encountered in activating and training people in prayer is teaching them how to pray proactive prayers instead of reactive prayers. The mindset of most intercessors is to pray after the fact to break the stronghold of the enemy. However, this type of theology has crippled as well as impaired the body of Christ from praying effective prayers. In Dr. Francis Myles' book, *The Spirit of Divine Interception*, he has meticulously addressed this type of myopic thinking along with redefining the original concept why God sent Jesus into the world. The misnomer of intervention can no longer be calibrated above interception. I recommend every prayer leader and pastor read this book. It is an invaluable resource tool in our continuous learning process." - Dr. Shirley K. Clark, Chancellor, Anointed For Business Leadership Institute, CEO, Clark's Consultant Group, National Prayer Coordinator, Rosa Parks Institute Protecting Freedom Prayer Initiative

....

"There is currently no spiritual technology more needed for the *'day to day'* lives of God's people than the Spirit of Interception. There is a scriptural text in the Bible that has puzzled so many believers over the years. It has done so because it was spoken by the Lord Jesus Christ Himself, yet believers have seemed to be unable to grasp the reality of its application. It is found in St. Luke 10:19.

'Behold, I give unto you power to tread on serpents and scorpions, and over all the power of the enemy: and nothing shall by any means hurt you.'

While the church has been able to grasp the concept of having power over demonic spirits it yet wrestles with the words *'and nothing shall by any means hurt you.'* Nearly every believer that you can speak to will have a testimony of how they have been under terrible attacks, only to wonder in bewilderment, why God hasn't prevented so many of them? In the technology of spiritual warfare it has been plausible and proven that we can discover and destroy the effects of demonic attacks and controlling spirits in the lives of believers. However, it has not been as easy to *'prevent'* these attacks from occurring. It has taken more than the quoting of Scripture texts and strong faith to intercept these attacks. There is an old saying that would be welcome in this case… *'an ounce of prevention is worth a pound of cure.'* What would it be like if we could prevent so many of these issues from occurring rather than expending tremendous amounts of spiritual energy and resources on the conversion of these circumstances? What will our lives be like when we learn how to apply the technology that enforces the words… *'and nothing shall by any means hurt you?'*

I believe that God has revealed this powerful technology called The Spirit of Interception. We've received a *'shadow'* of revelation about this in the past from very prominent texts in the Bible, yet we have not had a full disclosure of their application. One such text is found in *Isaiah 54:17:*

'No weapon that is formed against thee shall prosper; and every tongue that shall rise against thee in judgment thou shalt condemn. This is the heritage of the servants of the Lord, and their righteousness is of me, saith the Lord.'

Because of this tremendous revelation by my covenant brother Dr. Francis Myles, all of this has begun to change! We are walking in a brand new season of light concerning the power of protection that our High Priest Jesus Christ has provided for us through the tremendous covenant of the Order of Melchizedek. A working experiential knowledge of this great covenant will change much of the focus of our spiritual warfare.

It will express the true meaning of spiritual government and power as seen in *Isaiah 9:7. 'Of the increase of his government and peace there shall be no end.'* True peace is not experienced by warfare as much as it is experienced by the show of *'Pre-emptive Power.'* The increase of *'Peace'* is actually the result of an increase in *'Governmental power.'* Stronger governments have to do less to engage in shows of force than weaker governments who desire to give themselves a fighting chance by engaging in conflict with the hopes of catching the stronger government at a weak point. *'Pre-emptive Power'* is the stronger technology because it results in greater victories than frontal attacks between forces.

Dr. Myles' revelation is applicable to the lives of every believer. No matter what the race, creed, color or geographic location of the believer is, this technology is the answer to the problem that we all face. We have long waited for these answers. Thank God they have arrived!" - Dr. Gordon E. Bradshaw, Presiding Apostle, Global Effect Ministries Network

"Occasionally in life we meet individuals who impact us in a deeply profound way. These people redefine or reaffirm who God is to us and in us. Dr. Francis Myles has definitely been one of those voices of inspiration and revelation along my journey. Meeting Dr. Myles was certainly a Divine Interception in my life and I believe that the fact that you are reading this book is a Divine Interception for you as well.

In my work with InVision, my personal development company, we teach on the foundational concept of L.E.N.S. ™ which stands for, 'Life's Emotional Navigation Systems™.' Our LENSes are what dictate and drive our sub-conscious belief systems. And science says that those belief systems drive and affect over 95 percent of the decisions 'we think' we are making. We can then say that our LENSes act like onboard GPS systems. Wherever our subconscious destinations are pointed is where we ultimately end up in life. This is proven out in Proverbs 23:7, 'As a man thinks in his heart so is he.'

In our live seminars we engage people in games and activities where they can Discover, Remove and Smash their LENSes. It is a very effective way to truly discover what we think in the depths of our hearts versus what we think we believe in our head. It is so effective we make the promise at our seminars that our events will produce huge results in a short period of time. Yet, there is an even higher way than what we can just do in the natural. A way that if we are sensitive to the Spirit, can produce quantum shifts in not only the natural but supernatural realm as well.

That way is the technology of the Spirit of Divine Interception. In this book you will not only re-discover this ancient technology, you will also be given a set of practical steps to activate it in your life in profound ways. As Dr. Myles shares in this book, '*The Spirit of Interception is the Spiritual Technology that God uses to bring us to Him before the Devil can take us out.*' As I look back over my life, I see time and time again where God intercepted me. Sometimes I was aware of the interception and was immediately grateful. At other times it was in the midst of circumstances and events in my life that were traumatic or full of change and repositioning and I did not see His hand until many years later.

Recently my wife and I were at home discussing some past events of our lives that stemmed back almost two decades ago when we met in college. We were discussing a very traumatic event, and how it had affected us and almost everyone we knew at that time. In a moment in time, almost twenty years ago because of the acts of a few people, our whole world, our friends, and everything we thought we 'knew' changed.

Over the years we had viewed this event through a certain 'LENS' and thus the events had a certain meaning to us. Therefore, they produced certain emotions that did nothing but reinforce that LENS or belief. Yet, after reading Dr. Myles' book just a few days ago, in a split second with one change in viewpoint we saw something we had never seen before. We saw the technology of Interception and how God had taken us in right before the devil could take us out and how that one event had changed the course of our lives together for good.

As you read through this book I pray that the Holy Spirit will give you new eyes (LENSes) to see His hand guiding your life and new ears to hear His voice as He speaks to you and reminds you that He was speaking to you all along your journey even if you didn't think you were hearing Him. By viewing the event I discussed previously through a different set of LENSes it shifted my wife and me from a victim mentality to a victor. We had forgiven the situation long ago, yet we had framed what had happened based on our beliefs and also how we interpreted the circumstances. When the Lord showed us how, through the Spirit of Interception, He had taken us in before the Devil could take us out ... it changed EVERYTHING.

In our seminars we have an exercise that helps people shift from Victim to Victor in a very short period of time. It is a process and formula you can duplicate over and over again in your own home or with a spouse or friend once you have experienced it. Yet, after years of teaching this process, God still used our understanding of the Spirit of Interception to minister to my wife and me at a deeper level and showed us His interception not only at a soulish level but at a spiritual level as well.

God is in the business of restoration and fulfillment of destiny. And I believe Dr. Myles has re-discovered an ancient technology that will catapult all who embrace it into Kingdom Realm living. This is especially true for those, like many of us, who are called to Marketplace Ministry. God is bringing Kings together in the Marketplace to do exploits for Him. To do this, one of our secret weapons as Kingdom citizens is unity and being 'As One.' Jesus said that the world would know us based on our unity and love for one another. And the greatest way to do this is to come among other Kingdom citizens, like Jesus, as one who serves. To do this though, we have to be intercepted from the Babylonian ways of doing things and allow our hearts to be intercepted and circumcised by the King for His Kingdom.

The Spirit of Interception is just that type of technology... a divine technology of heart and spirit. Are you ready for the next level of Kingdom living and manifestation in your life? Then get ready for a Divine Interception that is going to redefine your past and reframe your future and propel you towards your destiny." - Kyle Newton, President & Founder of InVision, www.iCanInVision.com, Tribus - www.iTribus.com, Newton, Inc. - www.NewtonInc.com

the SPIRIT of DIVINE INTERCEPTION

...Rediscovering the Greatest Spiritual Technology on Earth

BY

DR. FRANCIS MYLES

The Spirit of Divine Interception

ISBN 9780615875484

All Scripture quotations are taken from the New Living Translation version of the Holy Bible unless indicated otherwise.

TABLE OF CONTENTS

FOREWORD

I am sensing a lot of excitement in the Lord's heart about this book. It is going to help many, many people and will be an answer to prayer for many others. This book is destined to become a classic and will help expose and break the negative cycles operating in some people and interrupt and short circuit demonic mechanisms and technologies.

This book will also help advance, accelerate and strengthen the convergence between intercession, prophetic and the marketplace as business leaders begin to understand better how important, essential and mission critical it is for them to hear from God both personally and corporately and to involve God in their business decisions and plans and to seek confirmation and guidance from others who are gifted, mature, wise and trustworthy in the things of the Spirit. Business, marriage, parenting and ministry are team sports.

Just as Sir Isaac Newton discovered the law of gravity and other notable scientists and inventors such as Albert Einstein have discovered other laws, properties, and secrets of the universe and how it functions, Dr. Francis Myles has uncovered through divine revelation a principle of how God operates that can bring us one step closer in our relationship with God, not only in our personal walk with God but in how we operate in business and the marketplace. As such, this is an important book on several levels—both theologically and practically. And God has chosen this time to restore this principle to the body of Christ. God is in the business of redeeming, and intercepting, the human race. He is the God of the universe while at the same time the God of the individual. He is impersonal and personal at the same time. He knows the number of hairs on our head and the needs and desires of our heart, while at the same time He is able to exercise mercy and judgment, as the case may be, on entire nations. This is a great mystery which is only revealed in and through His Son, Christ Jesus, and the atoning and finished work of Christ on the cross of Calvary to free us from the law and the bondage of sin and death.

It is said that "For by him [Christ] all things were created and...in him [Christ] all things hold together" (Col. 2:15-20) while at the same time Christ "ever lives to intercede for us" as a high priest after the Order of Melchizedek (Heb. 7:25). The premise of the popular television program

FOREWORD

Touched by an Angel was divine interception. We as mortals, made in the image of God but not yet clothed with immortality, need interception at various times in our lives for a variety of reasons. Some need interception in business or finance, some in a marriage or relationship, some for physical or emotional needs, some for religious or political persecution or tyranny, and some for salvation. God does not violate our free will, and gives us the power of choice at all times, but at the same time He does not abandon or forsake us, even when we are in rebellion or bondage or ignorance or religion. Omnipresence is part of the nature of God. He can be everywhere at once. He is always a heartbeat and a prayer away, and for those of us who have accepted Jesus Christ as Lord and Savior and been born again, the Holy Spirit lives within us. We are the modern day temples and tabernacles of God and He chooses to dwell among us and lives in our hearts.

Open yourself up to divine interception and learn to see the circumstances and events of your life through God's eyes. Interception is to be desired, prized and valued above intervention in the lives of individuals, families, churches, businesses, governmental agencies, organizations and nations just as God values obedience above sacrifice, and mercy above judgment. The first technology in each case is of a higher order than the latter. Your life and your destiny are not only about you, but about others. So ask God to increase and/or activate your gift of discernment, spiritual sensitivity and awareness. You'll be glad you did, and the results may surprise you.

Dr. Bruce Cook
Vice President of Kingdom Marketplace Coalition LLC
www.mykmcportal.com/brucecook
Founder of Kingdom Economic Yearly Summit (K.E.Y.S.)
www.kingdomeconomicsummit.com
President of Kingdom House Publishing
www.kingdomhousepublishing.com
President of VentureAdvisers, Inc. www.ventureadvisers.com
President of Glory Realm Ministries www.gloryrealm.net

PREFACE

"Men," he said, "I believe there is trouble ahead if we go on—shipwreck, loss of cargo, and danger to our lives as well." Acts 27:10

If you have never uttered these words: "I wish I had listened to my wife," "I wish I had listened to my gut-feeling," "I wish I had cashed out my stock options before the company went belly-up" or "Something in my heart told me not to do business or get in the car with him, but I failed to listen," then you probably live on the planet Mars in a space bubble millions of miles away from our broken down planet called Earth. The above expressions are very common expressions among earthlings. They are as universal as they are common.

Strategic and valuable business and personal relationships have suffered greatly behind many of these very common but painful expressions. Their universality and the spiritual, emotional and financial damage that they infer into the human experience betray a more sinister and diabolical conspiracy against God's inherent desire to see His eternal goodness mirrored in the human experience, both locally and globally.

"For I know the plans I have for you," says the LORD. "They are plans for good and not for disaster, to give you a future and a hope." Jeremiah 29:11

In view of God's inherent desire and expressed will to give all humanity a life of fulfilled dreams and realized hopes it behooves us to investigate the cause behind much of the suffering and loss that plagues the human experience. Many of these expressions of regret that we have alluded to demand further investigation into these common, but disastrous experiences with forensic aptitude. This book is an investigation into this spiritual phenomenon.

At the heart of all informed spiritual or scientific research is a body of questions that fuel the whole investigation. In the spirit of informed investigation, this book will seek to answer the following questions…

- Why are these questions of regret universal and common to the human experience?

- Is there a diabolical and calculated conspiracy behind many of the tears of regret that are common to the human experience?

- If God is good and all powerful, why does He allow the evil and pain of regret to be visited upon innocent people?

- Why do most people blame God for the pain in their lives that is a direct consequence of their actions?

- Why are these stories of disaster concentrated in the Marketplace?

- Is there a "fail-proof" technology for "intercepting" much of the evil that is visited upon humans before it actually happens?

The body of work in this book is dedicated to answering these six powerful questions. This book will also contain case studies from the Bible and from present day people that are designed to illustrate the dire need for a fail-proof spiritual technology for intercepting demonically engineered diabolical plans and ploys to inject suffering, loss and injury in the human experience.

This book is the fruit of the author's divinely orchestrated mandate to reveal to all seekers one of the greatest and most powerful spiritual technologies in all of creation. This ancient technology is so powerful and priceless that many of today's superpowers would spend all they had in their treasury to purchase the rights to such a powerful "fail-safe" technology. This ancient technology is called*... "The Technology of Divine Interception or the Spirit of Interception."*

This book will clearly demonstrate that in ALL cases of both pain and pleasure in the human experience, the Spirit of interception is either the missing or present ingredient. Unfortunately, more often than not, the technology of divine interception is usually absent in most decisions which are made by earthlings. This book will show that in the absence of this spiritual technology, demonic powers (the devil) have free course to do whatever they so desire. There is always the element of vicarious pain and suffering whenever demons find a spiritual environment where they can have full expression.

At the heart of this writing is an inherent desire by the author to unmask and destroy this free reign of demonic powers in the lives of Kingdom citizens. When the divorce rate among God's people is equal and sometimes higher than the world, there is serious cause for alarm. When stories of bad business deals between brothers and sisters in the Lord are as common as stories of bad business deals among the unsaved, there is serious cause for alarm. But further investigation will clearly show that in all of these cases the difference between marriages which ended in divorce and those that did not was the "Spirit of interception." The difference between business deals among Kingdom citizens that went belly-up and those which succeeded was also the "Spirit of interception."

This book will show and confirm that the greatest investment Kingdom entrepreneurs can ever make for themselves, in order to create a buffer against painful financial losses in the world of commerce, is in "understanding how the technology of divine interception" works. The technology of divine interception is the reason why King Solomon became the richest and wisest man who has ever lived. It is the reason why Saint Paul became the most powerful apostle in human history. It is the reason why millions of people who were hell bound became transformed into blood-washed children of the Most High God. Disobedience to this technology is the reason why the devil was able to enter into the heart of Judas Iscariot (Luke 22:1-4) and cause him to betray the sinless Son of God.

Since I am an apostle to Kingdom entrepreneurs, this book is written with my heartfelt desire to teach Kingdom entrepreneurs how to incorporate and employ the technology of divine interception in their vehicles of commerce. It saddens me to see the millions of dollars in Kingdom resources that are wasted in bad business deals, simply because many Kingdom entrepreneurs have never been trained to interface accurately with the technology of divine interception. The greatest item of loss in myriads of these business deals that went sour is the most priceless asset that God ever gave mankind. This priceless item is called "TIME!"

PREFACE

To every thing there is a season, and a time to every purpose under the heaven. Ecclesiastes 3:1

According to King Solomon, "TIME" is the instrument that God uses to measure out and execute His eternal purpose for His creation. Time and purpose are completely inseparable. You cannot waste one without wasting the other. When God's people or Kingdom entrepreneurs waste "TIME" in meaningless relationships or unfruitful business deals they are also wasting away their "PURPOSE." This is why Kingdom citizens must strive to understand and cooperate with this ancient spiritual technology of interception, so that they can "REDEEM" both their time and their purpose. If this book has found its way into your hands, it is because you have been chosen by God to become both a "recipient and custodian" of this ancient spiritual technology. YOU ARE ABOUT TO BE INTERCEPTED. It is my pleasure to LEAD you on this AMAZING JOURNEY OF DISCOVERY!

Yours for Kingdom Advancement,
Dr. Francis Myles
Founder and Chairman of Kingdom Marketplace Coalition LLC
Virtual Kingdom Boardroom LLC, Kingdom Marketplace
University LLC
Get your Groove on TV & Radio LLC
Senior Pastor, Breakthrough City Kingdom Embassy

CHAPTER ONE
A PARALLEL UNIVERSE

That same day Jesus was approached by some Sadducees—religious leaders who say there is no resurrection from the dead. They posed this question: ²⁴ "Teacher, Moses said, 'If a man dies without children, his brother should marry the widow and have a child who will carry on the brother's name.' ²⁵ Well, suppose there were seven brothers. The oldest one married and then died without children, so his brother married the widow. ²⁶ But the second brother also died, and the third brother married her. This continued with all seven of them. ²⁷ Last of all, the woman also died. ²⁸ So tell us, whose wife will she be in the resurrection? For all seven were married to her." ²⁹ Jesus replied, "Your mistake is that you don't know the Scriptures, and you don't know the power of God. Matthew 22:23-29

By definition the word "parallel" means "aligned, side-by-side." One of the fundamental truths of the Bible is that we live in a "parallel" universe. This means that no matter what we think we are not alone. Our earthly existence is a carbon copy of a higher life borrowed from the spirit world. Even though we live in a world that worships the human body we are actually spirit beings having a bodily experience.

TIMELESS PRINCIPLES

The explosion of new age phenomenon and teachings has caused many people to convince themselves that life is one-dimensional. They believe there is no life outside our present earthly existence. Nothing could be further from the truth and those who have believed this lie are in for a rude awakening. If we live our lives as though life is one-dimensional we are going to miss the divine messages that are coming to us from the spirit world. We will also fail to discern the diabolical intent of the demonic messages that are also proceeding from the underworld.

Imagine the shock that welcomes atheists in the other world when their earthly existence expires. It must be very depressing for them to realize that the God they had denied all their life actually exists and so does the devil. Discovering that we live in a parallel universe when you have already arrived in the portals of hell must be extremely depressing and frightening to say the least. In the blockbuster movie *The Gladiator*, Maximus, the commander of the northern armies of Rome, tells his troops before the battle for Germania with the barbarian horde this amazing statement; *"that what we do in life echoes in eternity!"*

> *The explosion of new age phenomena and teachings has caused many people to convince themselves that life is one-dimensional.*

No truer statement could have been spoken from a movie made in Hollywood. What we do in life does echo in eternity. The writer of the book of Ecclesiastes tells us that there is nothing new under the sun. Many would take offense at this statement. If asked, they would point to the many scientific and technological discoveries of our time as evidence to the contrary. This is because they fail to appreciate the deeper and prophetic meaning of this powerful verse from Scripture. King Solomon is not talking about scientific and technological discoveries; he is alluding to the timeless principles of God that govern our universe. *These timeless principles are eternal and as such transcend any new scientific and technological discovery.* This means that even when scientists discovered the law of gravity it was only new to them and not to God.

THE SCIENCE OF THE ANCIENTS

Since many ancient historical documents about the discoveries of past generations have been lost to our generation, we do not know how much of our present day discoveries had already been discovered by people of the ancient world. For instance, scientists and mathematicians are still trying to figure out the highly advanced scientific engineering behind the architectural designs of the Pyramids of Egypt. Both scientists and mathematicians agree that we have not yet rediscovered the lost science behind the building of the Pyramids of Egypt. What is obvious is that the science used to build the pyramids of ancient Egypt is very advanced and so I rest my case.

> *The thing that hath been, it is that which shall be; and that which is done is that which shall be done: and there is no new thing under the sun. [10]Is there any thing whereof it may be said, See, this is new? it hath been already of old time, which was before us. Ecclesiastes 1:9-10*

In Ecclesiastes 1:10 Solomon the preacher makes it clear that what we think is new has already been under a different dispensation of human government. This statement is not meant to discourage us from pursuing new discoveries. To the contrary, if we truly understand the real meaning of this powerful statement, we will passionately work to discover the timeless principles of God that have been lost on our generation. These divine timeless principles that are embedded within the matrix of creation that can both change our science and technology to help us better our lives in the present. The secret to unmasking or understanding Ecclesiastes 1:10 is to understand how this verse ties into Ecclesiastes 3:14.

> *And I know that whatever God does is final. Nothing can be added to it or taken from it. God's purpose is that people should fear*

him. Ecclesiastes 3:14

In Ecclesiastes 3:14 King Solomon tells us that whatever God does is final or lasts for ever and nothing can be added to it or taken from it. What does this mean? It means that all of God's timeless principles and laws that He has masterfully embedded in the matrix of creation can be depended upon to never change their specific and inherent behavior patterns once discovered. Consider this; if the law of gravity or the law of aerodynamics changed frequently in both behavior and pattern, how would we build anything stable around such fluctuating laws of nature? It would be practically impossible to attach any credible scientific and technological device to such unpredictable laws of nature.

The aviation industry would be nonexistent in a climate where the laws of gravity and aerodynamics changed frequently from studied behavior and patterns. Many of us would be walking hundreds of miles or driving thousands of miles to distant places, because it would be impossible to fly any airplane safely under such unpredictable conditions. But the preacher of righteousness tells us that *"whatever God does is final and nothing can be changed or added to it."* This means that the law of gravity or aerodynamics will behave the same way all the time and in every continent of the world. This then makes it easy to attach a scientific or technological device that can work around the complete stability and reliability of these timeless principles of God in creation. These timeless principles are so steadfast that they will work for the atheist and for those who believe in God.

You might be wondering why I'm spending so much time hammering this point into your mind; trust me there is reason behind the madness. The conclusion that I want us to come to is simply this; if physical laws of nature such as gravity and aerodynamics are so consistent and stable, what about spiritual laws which are much higher than the laws that govern the world of matter? *Natural laws control and govern the physical planet called Earth, while spiritual laws control and govern the invisible world.* If we discover a spiritual law or technology that God has embedded in the matrix of creation we know that we can bank on this spiritual law or technology to work exactly the same way, all the time and in every place. In a world that suffers from a lack of consistency, knowing that the timeless principles of God embedded into the matrix and fabric of creation can never change is truly satisfying and empowering at the same time.

> *Natural laws control and govern the physical planet called Earth, while spiritual laws control and govern the invisible world.*

About eight days later Jesus took Peter, John, and James up on a mountain to pray. [29] And as he was praying, the appearance of his face was transformed, and his clothes became dazzling white. [30] Suddenly, two men, Moses and Elijah, appeared and began talking with Jesus. [31] They were glorious to see. And they were speaking about his exodus from this world, which was about to be fulfilled in Jerusalem. Luke 9:28-31

You might be wondering why a book on divine interception starts out with a chapter on a parallel universe. I am glad you asked; let me give you the answer. The technology of divine interception is only possible on the human plane because our present world is governed by a very powerful invisible world. The supernatural intersection of our physical world of matter with that invisible world is what creates both the climate and conditions for divine interception.

To unmask this invisible world that governs our physical world of matter, Jesus Christ took three of his apprentice apostles, Peter, James and John to the famous mountain of transfiguration. At the summit of this historic mountain Jesus was supernaturally transfigured and the glory of a man saturated with divinity was made manifest before their very eyes. During this amazing time of the God encounter the patriarchs Moses and Elijah appeared in glorified bodies and began to minister to Christ about his death and resurrection.

When Peter saw this amazing phenomenon, he was so deeply moved by the supernatural intersection of our present world with that powerful invisible world of God, that he suggested they build three tents on top of the mountain and never go down to the valley below - one tent for Christ, one for Moses and one for the prophet Elijah. But Jesus would not have it. He allowed himself to be transfigured before His apprentice apostles to prove to them the reality of the Kingdom of God that they would be serving as New Testament apostles. He wanted them to know that at any given moment they were never far away from divine interception.

> *"Simon, Simon, Satan has asked to sift each of you like wheat.*
> *³² But I have pleaded in prayer for you, Simon, that your faith*
> *should not fail. So when you have repented and turned to me*
> *again, strengthen your brothers." ³³ Peter said, "Lord, I am ready*
> *to go to prison with you, and even to die with you." ³⁴ But Jesus*
> *said, "Peter, let me tell you something. Before the rooster crows*
> *tomorrow morning, you will deny three times that you even know*
> *me." Luke 22:31-34*

Perhaps one of the most striking moments of divine interception is found in Luke 22 when Jesus intercepted a diabolical conspiracy to destroy Peter's faith in God. Being a man of the Spirit, Jesus Christ had become privy to a demonic conspiracy that Satan was purposing against one of his dearest apostles. According to Scripture Jesus prayed against this demonically engineered attack against Peter from prospering. Without mincing his words, Jesus told Peter that Satan had asked to sift him like wheat but Christ had pleaded for his life before God.

Peter, being the person that he was, answered Christ back without thinking it through. Peter told the Lord that he would not fall to the devil and that he was willing to go to prison with Christ. But since Jesus was not passing out an opinion poll he simply stated as a matter of fact that before the rooster crowed once, Peter would have denied the Lord three times. But how did Christ intercept this demonically engineered conspiracy against Peter? The answer is amazingly simple. Jesus Christ had trained himself to live in both worlds simultaneously. He lived in this physical world of matter, but spiritually he lived in the supernatural world of God.

This is why we are admonished by the apostle Paul to live and walk in the spirit. The great apostle to the church also tells us to live by faith and not by sight. These apostolic concepts of living would be redundant if we did not live in a parallel universe. If our physical world was a one-dimensional world it would not make sense to ask people to live by faith. It makes more sense to live by sight in a purely physical world. But if we're living in a two-dimensional world with one world extremely superior to the other in both power and technology, it is only prudent to live by faith since faith is the currency of that invisible and superior world.

This book is about an ancient spiritual technology - a technology so potent demonic powers have no answer for it. If the devil was to gather every demon under his disposal to overthrow this spiritual technology he would fail miserably. This spiritual technology is a fail-safe technology. This means that in the absence of human error or disobedience the technology that this book is built around can never fail!

What spiritual technology am I referring to? *This special technology is called the technology of divine interception.* It is a technology because like all technologies it is the science of improvement. It is a technology because like all technologies it follows a predictable pattern of systems and protocols. It is a technology because like all technologies it is 100 percent user-friendly and can be mass duplicated to meet the needs of a growing audience. It is a technology because it follows a set of unchangeable governing laws.

Jesus Christ had trained himself to live in both worlds simultaneously. He lived in this physical world of matter but spiritually he lived in the supernatural world of God.

In this book we'll attempt to describe and analyze this powerful ancient technology in detail. This book will show you a number of things including: the anatomy of this spiritual technology and how it functions in real-time, how this technology can change your life and business for the greater good, how to cooperate with the technology of divine interception to thwart the activity of demonic powers, how to recognize when God has initiated this technology in your life or vehicle of commerce, and how the invisible world is connected to the visible world at the place the ancients called the place of INTERCEPTION.

LIFE APPLICATION SECTION

MEMORY VERSE

That same day Jesus was approached by some Sadducees—religious leaders who say there is no resurrection from the dead. They posed this question: ²⁴ "Teacher, Moses said, 'If a man dies without children, his brother should marry the widow and have a child who will carry on the brother's name.' ²⁵ Well, suppose there were seven brothers. The oldest one married and then died without children, so his brother married the widow. ²⁶ But the second brother also died, and the third brother married her. This continued with all seven of them. ²⁷ Last of all, the woman also died. ²⁸ So tell us, whose wife will she be in the resurrection? For all seven were married to her." ²⁹ Jesus replied, "Your mistake is that you don't know the Scriptures, and you don't know the power of God. Matthew 22:23-29

REFLECTIONS

Do we or do we not live in a Parallel Universe?

_____

_____

_____

_____

_____

_____

How does living in a Parallel Universe help facilitate the Technology of Divine Interception?

_____

_____

_____

JOURNAL YOUR THOUGHTS

_____
_____
_____
_____
_____
_____
_____
_____
_____
_____
_____
_____
_____
_____
_____
_____
_____
_____
_____
_____
_____
_____
_____
_____
_____
_____
_____
_____
_____
_____
_____
_____

A PARALLEL UNIVERSE

CHAPTER TWO
DISASTERS IN COMMERCE

I have a special love for businessmen and women. I believe that God has called me as an apostle to marketplace leaders. After the release of my seminal book *The Order of Melchizedek*, the Holy Spirit spoke to me and said, *"Son I have called you to awaken the spirit of the corporate Joseph in the nations."* This statement from the Holy Spirit is what led me to launch our company Kingdom Marketplace Coalition LLC (KMC) – a company dedicated to networking and training Josephs within the greater body of Christ through our business, education and social networking portal (www.mykmcportal.com).

I really believe that God has called me to teach and train marketplace leaders how to take dominion over and occupy the seven mountains of culture. I particularly love the mountain of business because it employs millions of people around the world. But the time I have spent with many Kingdom businessmen and women has proven to me that there is a dire need for the technology of divine interception in the world of commerce. There are a lot of hurting businessmen and women in the marketplace because of failed business ventures.

WOUNDED JOSEPHS AND DANIELS

I've sat across the table in counseling sessions with several businessmen and women while they recounted to me the bad and painful business deals that they have been a part of. Some of these Josephs and Daniels have lost their wives and families in the process of doing business. One of the Josephs I am mentoring lost $30 million dollars in a bad business deal that left him and his family in financial ruins. Currently he is on the pathway toward recovery but it has been a slow and painful process.

He told me that after he discovered that two of his business partners had been stealing the money that they had all invested together in their airline and were dumping the money into a shell corporation they had formed without his knowledge, he was very devastated. The most difficult part of this whole ordeal was telling his wife and children that they had lost $30 million dollars of the money they had saved up for their future together. For all practical purposes they had been reduced to zero and had to start from scratch. By God's grace I have never lost $30 million but I can imagine it is a very painful and devastating loss.

Stories of such monstrous losses in bad business deals by Kingdom entrepreneurs is the reason why the Holy Spirit commissioned me to write this book. The pain and loss associated with many of these bad business deals speaks to the dire need for a fail-proof spiritual technology that can help marketplace ministers avoid many of these painful losses. This book is about identifying that spiritual technology. Throughout this writing we will identify this technology as *"the technology of divine interception."* But before we dissect this ancient technology in greater detail, we will first examine biblical and real-life case studies of disasters in commerce that took place in the absence of this technology.

We struggled along the coast with great difficulty and finally arrived at Fair Havens, near the town of Lasea. [9] We had lost a lot of time. The weather was becoming dangerous for sea travel because it was so late in the fall, and Paul spoke to the ship's officers about it. [10] "Men," he said, "I believe there is trouble ahead if we go on—shipwreck, loss of cargo, and danger to our lives as well." [11] *But the officer in charge of the prisoners listened more to the ship's captain and the owner than to Paul. Acts 27:8-12*

One of the greatest disasters in commerce happened in Acts chapter 27 when Paul the Apostle was being transported to Rome as a prisoner. The apostle Paul and a band of other prisoners were placed aboard a cargo ship bound for Rome. It goes without saying that a cargo ship is a vehicle of commerce that is used to transport merchandise for other corporations to distant shores. On this journey bound for Rome they experienced some very bad weather; as a result they lost a lot of time getting to their destination.

There is a dire need for the technology of divine interception in the world of commerce. There are a lot of hurting businessmen and women in the marketplace.

Every businessman and woman that I've ever met is very conscientious of time. This is because time in business equals money; hence the proverbial saying *"time is money."* I can imagine that the CEO of the cargo ship Paul was on was under pressure to get to Rome on time. *The only problem is that pressure is not a good leader in business. Business decisions made under pressure usually never turn out to be right.* This is why when I am mentoring Kingdom businessmen and women, I teach them on the importance of *"operating in the principle of rest"* when making major business decisions. Here is what I tell them, "do not be led by pressure; be led by God!"

THE VOICE OF DIVINE INTERCEPTION

Even though the apostle Paul was a prisoner on this cargo ship he was still a high-ranking ambassador of the Kingdom of God nevertheless. When he spoke from his lofty position as a Kingdom ambassador his words carried tremendous weight in both the natural and spiritual worlds.

DISASTERS IN COMMERCE

Being a man of the spirit the apostle Paul could sense that their journey toward Rome would end in disaster if they forced their way through the bad weather. Paul spoke to the Roman commander who had custody over him that if they proceeded any further their journey would result in shipwreck and loss of cargo.

The Roman commander took Paul's warning to the owner and captain of the ship. Both the owner and captain of the ship sneered in contempt at Paul's admonition. They felt that they were more qualified to speak to the conditions at hand than a prisoner bound for Rome. They felt they were more experienced at the task of driving a ship through bad weather than Paul was giving them credit for. As such what was meant to be a moment of divine interception to prevent great loss was overturned by pride and disobedience. What the CEO of the cargo ship did not know was that Paul the Apostle was being used as a vehicle to manifest one of the most powerful spiritual technologies for avoiding loss in life and in commerce. God had chosen to use Paul as a vehicle of the technology of divine interception.

When a light wind began blowing from the south, the sailors thought they could make it. So they pulled up anchor and sailed close to the shore of Crete. [14] But the weather changed abruptly, and a wind of typhoon strength (called a "northeaster") burst across the island and blew us out to sea. [15] The sailors couldn't turn the ship into the wind, so they gave up and let it run before the gale. Acts 27:13-15

Since they had refused to heed his advice the apostle Paul resigned himself to their fate. Paul knew that no human being, nation or vehicle of commerce can ignore the technology of divine interception and get away with it. Paul also knew that demonic powers would quickly rally around the owner of the ship's disobedience to bring devastation to the cargo ship that Paul was traveling on. Acts 27 verse 13 seems to suggest that demonic powers were baiting the owner of the cargo ship that Paul was traveling on to move from their place of safety. The Bible says that a light wind began blowing from the south that deceived the ship captain and his crew of sailors into thinking that the weather was changing for the better. Nothing could have been further from the truth.

> *The only problem is that pressure is not a good leader in business. Business decisions made under pressure usually never turn out to be right.*

THE DEVIL IS BAITING YOU

Once the captain of the ship took the ship out of its God ordained place of safety where they were currently docked, they were quickly blindsided by an unforeseen hurricane. The weather became severe in a very short time and they were unable to go back to the place where they had previously docked. Suddenly Paul's admonition did not seem far-fetched anymore. I'm sure the owner of the cargo ship was probably slapping himself for not listening to Paul. He knew that besides placing his own company at risk, he had also placed the merchandise of his customers at very high risk. He knew that shipwreck would put him out of business and in debt to many of his customers.

The next day, as gale-force winds continued to batter the ship, the crew began throwing the cargo overboard. [19] The following day they even took some of the ship's gear and threw it overboard. [20] The terrible storm raged for many days, blotting out the sun and the stars, until at last all hope was gone. Acts 27:18-20

The hurricane force winds that surrounded the ship continued to batter the cargo ship that Paul was traveling on so much that the crew began to throw the ship's cargo overboard. Imagine how the owner of the ship must have felt when he saw the precious merchandise of his customers being thrown off the ship. He knew that his days in the shipping business were over. And all of this disaster in his vehicle of commerce could be traced to his inability and unwillingness to cooperate with the technology of divine interception when God initiated it. There are many Kingdom businessmen and women who have lost untold millions of dollars because they failed to respond to the technology of divine interception.

No one had eaten for a long time. Finally, Paul called the crew together and said, "Men, you should have listened to me in the

first place and not left Crete. You would have avoided all this
damage and loss. Acts 27:21

The severe weather on the treacherous seas became so serious that the crew of experienced sailors lost all hope of recovery. They could taste and smell the sentence of death upon their lives. They lost hope of coming out of the sea alive. As this atmosphere of somberness and depression descended upon the ship's crew and prisoners alike, Paul the Apostle rose up to speak. Without mincing his words the apostle Paul rebuked the owner of the ship and his captain for not heeding his warning. The apostle Paul told them that had they listened to him they would have avoided the damage to the ship and the loss of precious cargo. May Paul's warning to the CEO of the cargo ship serve as a lesson for Kingdom entrepreneurs who have not yet learned the art of cooperating with the technology of divine interception in their vehicle of commerce.

WHEN POWER CHANGES HANDS

But take courage! None of you will lose your lives, even though
the ship will go down. ²³ *For last night an angel of the God to*
whom I belong and whom I serve stood beside me, ²⁴ *and he*
said, 'Don't be afraid, Paul, for you will surely stand trial before
Caesar! What's more, God in his goodness has granted safety to
everyone sailing with you.' Acts 27:22-24

Knowing that the ship's crew of sailors and his fellow prisoners were completely despondent, the apostle Paul went on to deliver a message of hope from the throne of God. He told them to take courage and not lose hope. He told them that God had sent him an angel who had told him that none of them would lose their lives even though the ship itself would be lost. He told them that an angel of God had visited him with this powerful message from God. The angel of the Lord told Paul that he was not going to die on the ship because God wanted him to stand trial before Caesar. The angel of the Lord also told Paul that God was going to preserve the lives of all the men on the ship for his sake. Now, this is what I call having stature with God. This is why I encourage Kingdom entrepreneurs to be connected to the apostolic covering of a bona fide apostle or prophet of God. *Celebrating and embracing the foundational ministries of apostles and prophets can bring the climate of divine interception to many vehicles of commerce.* This is why God is restoring the ministries of apostles and prophets in the global church to give end-time Josephs and Daniels, Esthers and Lydias, proper spiritual covering for their marketplace mantles.

> *So take courage! For I believe God. It will be just as he said.*
> *²⁶ But we will be shipwrecked on an island."³⁰ Then the sailors tried to abandon the ship; they lowered the lifeboat as though they were going to put out anchors from the front of the ship. ³¹ But Paul said to the commanding officer and the soldiers, "You will all die unless the sailors stay aboard." ³² So the soldiers cut the ropes to the lifeboat and let it drift away. Acts 27:25-32*

Paul continued his ambassadorial address to the crew of sailors and to his fellow prisoners by telling them that he believed God would do exactly what he had promised him. When the sailors tried to abandon the ship by jumping into a lifeboat, Paul told the commanding officer that if they got out of the ship they would die. The commanding officer, having learned from his past mistake of not listening to Paul, did not want to make the same mistake twice. He quickly cut the ropes to the lifeboat. This time, the commanding officer cooperated with the technology of divine interception that God was initiating through Paul the second time around. *Sometimes God will allow us to suffer loss so that we can learn the importance of cooperating with the technology of divine interception when He initiates it.*

Celebrating and embracing the foundational ministries of apostles and prophets can bring the climate of divine interception to many vehicles of commerce.

> *Just as day was dawning, Paul urged everyone to eat. "You have been so worried that you haven't touched food for two weeks," he said. ³⁴ "Please eat something now for your own good. For not a hair of your heads will perish." ³⁵ Then he took some bread, gave*

thanks to God before them all, and broke off a piece and ate it.
[36] Then everyone was encouraged and began to eat—[37] all 276 of
us who were on board. [38] After eating, the crew lightened the ship
further by throwing the cargo of wheat overboard. Acts 27:33-38

This story from the book of Acts is one of my favorite biblical case studies on the importance of cooperating with the technology of divine interception in the marketplace. The story of pain and devastation that is covered in this passage of Scripture should give every marketplace minister reason to pause and reflect. This story shows us that having the necessary business skills and academic credentials is no substitute for having access to the technology of divine interception. I know many businessmen and women who lost thousands of dollars in business deals that they thought were going to pay them huge dividends. This is why having access to the supernatural is very critical to Kingdom businessmen and women. There are too many demonic technologies that are operating in the Earth's spiritual climate that demand Kingdom citizens to live in the supernatural dimensions of God.

A MERGER FROM HELL

One of my spiritual daughters, whom I will call Suzanne (not her real name) for the purpose of this real-life case study, told me a very sobering story. Suzanne and her father, who was also a pastor of a church, started a design company. This design company was dedicated to helping churches decorate their sanctuaries in a spirit of excellence. The company quickly became very successful in a very short time. God's hand of blessing was undeniable; He blessed everything they did.

The amazing success of their design company led them to Wall Street. They took their church design company public. Immediately after going public the value of their company rose to a stunning $17 million. Life was really looking up for them. They felt like God had kept His end of the bargain when He declares in His word that *"I am the God who gives you the power to make wealth," (Deut. 8:18).* As they say in the language of the streets they were flowing in the dough. But their stunning success would be short-lived because they had missed one moment of divine interception.

Suzanne and her father took on a new business partner, to help them go public. Their new business partner was also a professing Christian. They brought him on board because he was skilled in the process of turning private companies into publicly traded companies. This man had a very powerful gift of gab and knew how to talk church. He spoke the Christian language (Christianese) they wanted to hear, but there was a demonic technology which was operating in his soul that they completely ignored. Suzanne told me that she could pick up on the warning signs. The man was too smooth in his speech. She could sense there was falseness about him that she could not pinpoint accurately. But her father whom she loved and adored was taken up with this man. In her father's eyes this man was the hero that was going to make their company explode into the horizon.

> *Sometimes God will allow us to suffer loss so that we can learn the importance of cooperating with the technology of divine interception when he initiates it.*

In one sense her father was right. This new business partner that they had taken in was definitely going to make their company explode, but not in the manner they both expected. This new business partner cooked up the partnership agreement that he signed with them. In the middle of the contract he hid the fact that in the process of taking their company public, they were also signing the company over to him. Suzanne and her father were only too happy to have a brilliant Christian businessman join the team and they forgot to read the fine print. *I always tell Kingdom businessmen and women that the devil is always in the details and God always keeps things simple.*

Before long their new business partner began to manifest his demonic tendencies. He begun to systematically frustrate and undermine their efforts to grow their design company. This man managed to systematically frustrate them to the point where he forced them out of their own company. Suzanne told me that one morning she came to work at the company which she had started with her father, only to find that her executive office desk had been cleaned out. She had been fired. There was a pink slip on her desk. She felt like the earth had bottomed out under her feet and she felt like she was falling into a bottomless pit of despair. She walked out of the company that she and her father had founded in total shock. She could not believe that it was over. They had lost their inheritance (business) to a man who spoke the language of "Christianese."

She walked out of her executive offices with a box containing her belongings while her former employees looked on sheepishly. This was not the storybook ending that this merger was supposed to provide. This could have been a script taken out of a horror movie, not out of a business merger involving a so-called Christian brother. But life has very few storybook endings unless God is the one leading and writing the story.

Suzanne told me, "Dr. Myles, throughout the process of this merger I had a constant tugging on my heart. There was a growing restlessness in my spirit that I never shared with my father. I was afraid that since I was the only woman on the board if I resisted the merger I would have been labeled a Jezebel. So I kept silent." Well, her silence cost them millions of dollars and a company that they had founded from scratch. Over ten years later Suzanne and her father are still trying to recover financially. How is that for stale bread?

I always tell Kingdom businessmen and women that the devil is always in the details and God always keeps things simple.

ANALYZING THE ROOT PROBLEM

So what is that tugging at the heart or the restlessness in her spirit that she failed to respond to? It is the technology of divine interception. God in his eternal goodness, knowing the end from the beginning, was trying to intercept a demonic conspiracy to destroy her inheritance. God knew that in their particular case everything that was glittering was not gold, and it definitely was not God either. God was initiating the technology of divine interception in order to prevent the loss of millions of dollars in resources and the accompanying emotional devastation that came with this demonic package. But her disobedience or her fear shut down one of the most powerful spiritual technologies in all of creation. It is not that God failed her, but she failed God. Not a day goes by that she doesn't think she should have shared her misgivings about this man who destroyed their family's fortune.

But as the saying goes *"hindsight is more powerful than foresight."* May I submit to you that hindsight is only more powerful than foresight when we ignore what God is showing us about the future destiny. The more Kingdom citizens master the covenant of total obedience to God we will rediscover that foresight is more powerful than hindsight. This is why the Holy Spirit commissioned me to write this book. This book will also intercept the technology of disobedience that is very active in the lives of so many of God's children.

THE COVENANT

When God told me to write this book He came into a living covenant with me concerning this book. This is what God told me *"Son if you write this book exactly as I tell you to write it, I will intercept millions of lives and millions of dollars in Kingdom resources."* My dear friend this "Covenant" that God made with me is the driving engine behind the book you are now holding in your hands. It is a very powerful and living covenant with a God who does not lie. I believe that the only reason why you are holding this book in your hands is because God has set you up for divine interception. Get ready to be INTERCEPTED!

I decree that you shall not lose what God has given you as an inheritance. I decree and declare that you shall PURSUE, OVERTAKE and RECOVER ALL without fail (1 Sam. 30). I decree and declare that what the Lord Jesus Christ did for Peter, He will do for you in this prophetic season of destiny. He will supernaturally intercept Satan's desire to sift you like wheat. I decree and declare that the Holy Spirit is defusing every demonically engineered diabolical conspiracy against you. I decree and declare that the Holy Spirit through your obedience will quickly build a supernatural climate of divine interception around you.

> *I submit to you that hindsight is only more powerful than foresight when we ignore what God is showing us about the future destiny.*

A PERSONAL DISASTER

Awhile back my wife and I were guests in the beautiful home of one of our dear friends who pastors a thriving church in Tulsa, Oklahoma. She is a well-known national and international prophetess. We were sitting in her gorgeous kitchen, talking about things pertaining to the Kingdom of God.

Suddenly the presence of the Lord came upon her and she gave me that "prophetic bull's-eye look," which seemed to be saying, *"Francis, God wants to talk to you, now!"* She started to prophesy into my life and here is part of the prophecy she gave me from the Spirit of God... *"God has called you to teach the Body of Christ roots and origins. Many people in the Body of Christ do not like roots and origins, but you do, says the Lord. God is going to use you to show the Body of Christ that if the roots and origins of something they are doing are satanic, they cannot make them godly no matter what they do to them!"*

ROOTS AND ORIGINS

When I left her house, what she had prophesied to me was ringing in my spirit like a fire alarm which had been set off by the presence of a consuming fire. All I kept hearing in my spirit were the words, *"You have been called to teach the Body of Christ roots and origins."* Suddenly God was all over me like a mother chicken hovers over her eggs. He started conversing with me. God began to show me some of my past experiences—both good and bad. God showed me how everything that I have gone through was skillfully designed to bring me to a place where

I could experientially and conceptually understand the type of call that God had placed upon my life. The prophecy I had just received brought focus to what has always been in my life, but was somehow hidden from me.

God spoke to my spirit and said, *"Son I have surely called you to teach the Body of Christ about the roots and origins of divine and demonic technologies and how they work!"* As the light of God's glory exploded in my spirit, I started to see some of my past experiences in a new light. I was amazed to see the handwriting of God even on some very painful experiences that I had gone through. I will share with you one of those experiences, and hope it will shed light on the subject of roots and origins and how they affect us in the realm of the Spirit.

In October 2002, my wife and I flew to Malaysia to attend a school of ministry hosted by Dr. Jonathan David. At this school Dr. Jonathan David called my wife and I out of about a hundred pastors who had gathered from all over the world. He started to prophesy over us. The heart of the prophetic word was, *"God is calling you to plant a church."*

When we flew back to the United States, we began planning our church plant. We were living in Oklahoma City at the time. Around this same time, a woman from Chicago who had attended one of my revival services there, called me. She asked me when I was going to start a church in Chicago. Judging from how well-attended my Chicago conferences had been in the past, I knew I had an adequate following in the city of Chicago. So I took the call from this woman as a sign from God to start a church in Chicago. *But as soon as I announced to my wife that we were moving to Chicago, a strange uneasiness crept into my spirit.* Unfortunately I ignored the uneasiness that was building inside my spirit and explained it away as simply the fear of moving across state lines. How I wish this was the case.

> *Sometimes God will allow us to suffer loss so that we can learn the importance of cooperating with the technology of divine interception when he initiates it.*

DISASTERS IN COMMERCE

When we arrived in Chicago, things started to go wrong almost immediately. First and foremost the house we moved into was shrouded in a bitter legal controversy. The self-professing Christian real estate agent who had found us the house conveniently forgot to tell us that the house we were moving into was already in foreclosure proceedings.

Secondly, our new church plant was not growing as fast as we had anticipated. What's more, the Chicago businesswoman who had called to ask us to start a church in Chicago, only attended one of our church services, and then disappeared. The church offerings were terribly low, so I was forced to attack our savings to support us and a church that I had started in the power of the flesh. Within a couple of months we had exhausted our savings and things were getting desperate. The increased spiritual tension coupled with the ensuing financial crisis caused my wife and me to start arguing a lot. Our home was a not a home of peace during that short but painful excursion to Chicago.

In the midst of all of this housing and marital turmoil, the same uneasiness I had felt before we left Oklahoma City grew stronger. The mounting spiritual uneasiness robbed me of the little bit of joy I got out of the dismal successes we were experiencing in the growth of the new church plant. In my spirit I kept hearing God say things like, *"You are not supposed to be here. This is not the place I have called you to. No matter what you do here My blessing on your life will be limited at best!"*

In desperation I called Dr. Jonathan David in Malaysia, whom I highly respect as a true prophet of God and father in the faith. I asked him, in reverse, to pray and see if I was supposed to be in Chicago. He agreed and told me to call him back within two weeks.

During those two weeks I prayed and repented a gazillion times for having missed God. I was desperate. *I was begging God to reconsider and bless what I was doing in Chicago.* I negotiated with God desperately and asked Him to remember just how sincere my heart was in my service to Him. My efforts to move on God to change His mind fell on deaf ears because my predicament had nothing to do with how pure and sincere my heart was before God. Instead it had everything to do with the *spiritual roots and origins* of the church I was asking Him to bless.

> *God is going to use you to show the Body of Christ that if the roots and origins of something they are doing are satanic, they cannot make them godly no matter what they do to them!*

When the two weeks were up, I called Dr. David and asked him to tell me what God had told him. He said that God had told him that *"if I stayed in Chicago I would be able to build the church, but I would always struggle."* He went on to tell me that while he was praying for me, he *"saw a vision of a throne of glory rising out of the state of Texas"* and the Lord told him that *"the church which He had called me to build was in Texas and not Chicago!"*

God also told him that if I moved to Texas, God would give me a great church and a spiritual base from which my ministry would have a lasting impact on the whole United States. When I got off the phone with him, I knew I had a huge decision to make. The church I was leading in Chicago had now grown to about thirty-four members. It did not take much time to make my decision. God allowed the devil to overplay his hand to show me the dangerous position I was in, in the realm of the Spirit.

On a rainy and icy day, I decided to drive to Calumet City to visit some pastor friends of mine. I stopped at a traffic light. When it turned green, I quickly made my turn and I was horrified to see that heading right for me in my lane at a very high speed was a huge emergency ambulance truck, coming directly toward my small Mitsubishi Gallant!

If I have ever smelled death, I truly smelled it that day. Out of sheer panic and chemical reflex, I swerved to the right to get out of harm's way and collided head-on with a stationary car that was waiting for the traffic light to turn green on the opposite side of the street. The big emergency ambulance truck missed my small car by inches. My small car was a wreck, but I was alive, without any scratches. I was terrified. The Spirit of God spoke to my heart and said, *"If you do not leave Chicago, you will surely die here!"*

DISASTERS IN COMMERCE

I called my wife and told her we were leaving Chicago. I told her that I was going to close the church we had started. She was very relieved. When Sunday came I humbly stood before our church members and asked for their forgiveness for misleading them and thinking that I could be their spiritual shepherd outside the perfect will of God. I told them that I had founded the church on a spirit of rebellion to the inner witness of the Holy Spirit, who had tried to warn me not to leave Oklahoma City. At the time I did not know that no human being can ignore the technology of divine interception without paying a heavy price.

I told them that no matter how sincere I was or they were in our service to God, God was not going to place His complete blessing on our church. This is because the true spiritual roots and origins of our church-plant were based upon a spirit of rebellion to God's authority! I begged them to forgive me and to release me from the responsibility of being their pastor—they did, with tears of regret. The people wept bitterly because they truly loved my wife and me. Seeing their tears of regret made me even more determined to get back into God's perfect will for my life, so they could also discover theirs. This painful experience taught me the seriousness of *spiritual roots and origins* in the Kingdom of God. I also did not know that God was preparing me to write a book titled *The Spirit of Divine Interception*.

The reason I am telling you my disaster story is to let you know that I am no stranger to the painful consequences of violating the technology of divine interception, when God initiates it. Like many of you reading this book, I have been at the receiving end of the rewards of disobedience to this ancient technology of God. I also have my own diary of bad business deals that cost me dearly when I ignored the technology of divine interception. Perhaps this might be one of the reasons why God chose me to write this book. It is my hope and prayer that my story would become the interception point for many of you reading this book who are fixing to make a colossal mistake. Some mistakes can have disastrous consequences that can impose upon your life many years of suffering that God never intended you to endure.

LIFE APPLICATION SECTION

MEMORY VERSE

We struggled along the coast with great difficulty and finally arrived at Fair Havens, near the town of Lasea. [9] We had lost a lot of time. The weather was becoming dangerous for sea travel because it was so late in the fall, and Paul spoke to the ship's officers about it.[10] "Men," he said, "I believe there is trouble ahead if we go on—shipwreck, loss of cargo, and danger to our lives as well." [11] But the officer in charge of the prisoners listened more to the ship's captain and the owner than to Paul. Acts 27:8-12

REFLECTIONS

1. Why are there so many disasters in commerce, in the marketplace?

_____
_____
_____
_____
_____
_____

Please explain how the Technology of Divine Interception can prevent many of these bad business deals in the Marketplace?

_____
_____
_____
_____
_____
_____

DISASTERS IN COMMERCE

JOURNAL YOUR THOUGHTS

CHAPTER THREE
L.E.N.S. AND F.I.L.T.E.R.S.

In this section we will examine factors that hinder men and women from responding to the technology of divine interception at the subconscious and heart level. What we will examine in this passage is what I call the hidden factors and inherent genetic traits that impact human behavior and shape our view of the world around us. We will be dealing with lenses and filters that impact our ability to respond or not respond to the technology of divine interception when God initiates it.

In 2009, my wife and I and a couple of our leaders from my church (www.breakthroughcity.com) attended a very life-changing seminar hosted by a company called InVision Inc, which was founded by one of my favorite spiritual protégés and business partners by the name of Kyle Newton. I have been to several self development seminars, but I'd never been to one that was as impactful on the subconscious level as the "Awakening Seminars" hosted by Kyle Newton and InVision Inc. During the seminar Kyle introduced us to the concept called L.E.N.S. and how lenses affect our perception of the world. Then he made a very startling announcement that we all had lenses, and it was our job to discover whether our lenses gave us an accurate view of the world or a distorted view of the world around us. According to Kyle:

L.E.N.S. AND F.I.L.T.E.R.S.

"In my work with InVision, my personal development company, we teach on the foundational concept of L.E.N.S. ™ which stands for, **"Life's Emotional Navigation Systems ™."** Our L.E.N.S.es are what dictate and drive our sub-conscious belief systems. And science says that those belief systems drive and affect over 95 percent of the decisions "we think" we are making. We can then say that our L.E.N.S.es act like internal GPS systems. Wherever our subconscious destinations are pointed is where we ultimately end up in life. This is proven in Proverbs 23:7, *"As a man thinks in his heart so is he."* In our live seminars we engage people in games and activities where they can discover, remove and smash their L.E.N.S.es. It is a very effective way to truly discover what we think in the depths of our hearts versus what we think we believe in our head."

L.E.N.S.es AND F.I.L.T.E.R.S.

Before diving deeper into this discussion about lenses and filters we must first define these two phenomena.

L.E.N.S.es deal with how we SEE or THINK through things on the subconscious level. Lenses color how we see or think through things. This means that every human being's worldview is deeply affected and driven by the lenses they have on. We all have lenses, but the critical issue is whether our lenses have been compromised or contaminated by the things we have been through that are contrary to the word of God. Even though everybody has lenses, lenses have a special effect on men, because men are logical thinkers by nature. This is why most men that I know are relationally retarded because they like to analyze everything.

> *L.E.N.S.es deal with how we SEE or THINK through things on the subconscious level. F.I.L.T.E.R.S. deal with how we FEEL our way through things.*

When I got married I went through great frustration for a season, because whenever my wife told me anything that she was going through, I began to analyze it immediately. You can imagine where that landed me - somewhere in a shark infested ocean between the United States and Africa. I really thought she was asking me for a logical solution to her dilemma. My analytical mind quickly went to work to find the best possible logical solutions until I saw her looking at me like I'd lost my mind. It took me a while to realize that my wife was not looking for a logical solution to the problem. She just wanted me to know how she felt. It took me a while to realize that I approached life through my analytical lenses, while my wife approached life through her emotional filters.

F.I.L.T.E.R.S.™ (Feelings In Life Trigger Emotional Reactions Spontaneously™) deal with how we FEEL our way through things on a heart level. Filters color how we FEEL our way through things. This means that every human being's worldview is deeply affected and driven by the filters they have over their heart. We all have filters, but the critical issue is whether our filters have been compromised or contaminated by the things we have been through that are contrary to the word of God. Even though everybody has filters, filters have a special effect on women, because women are very relational by nature. This is why most women I know are relationship experts because they like to FEEL their way through things.

Since most women are born with highly sensitive, God-given filters, they can become the best vehicles of divine interception for their husband and children. I have stopped counting the number of times that men have told me they would not have lost the money or the business that they lost had they listened to their wife. I knew exactly how they felt, because I've said the same things to myself a couple of times. But the challenge most men have is that many women's filters have become compromised or contaminated over time through the disappointments and hurts they have been through.

Like the air filter next to the engine of a motor vehicle, sometimes our emotional filters get dirty or clogged with the wounds and traumas of life and then our spiritual engines do not run as efficiently or smoothly as they were designed to. Our emotional filters have to be cleaned or changed every so often and it is important to have regular spiritual check-ups or maintenance with a trusted spiritual leader, pastor, elder, or counselor as the case may be. King David prayed *"Test me O Lord and try me, examine my heart and my mind"* (Ps. 26:2). This is like saying, *"God please show me my filters and lenses. "* On another occasion David prayed *"Search me, O God, and know my heart; test me and know my anxious thoughts. See if there is any offensive way in me, and lead me in the way everlasting"* (Ps. 139:23-24). We should pray likewise periodically.

For many women the contamination of their God-given filters is usually tied to a dysfunctional relationship with their father in their childhood or an abusive boyfriend or other male relative. It is common knowledge that the most important relationship that every little girl longs for is a dynamic and vibrant relationship with her daddy. Every little girl wants to know that she is "Snow White" in her daddy's world. She wants to know that she is daddy's little princess. *A woman's relationship with her father establishes her identity, and how she FEELS about herself.* The difference between men and women is that men dress up to look handsome but women don't care about that. When a woman dresses up, she is not as concerned about looking great as much as she's concerned about FEELING that she's beautiful.

We cannot cover this important subject in great detail within the scope of this writing, but it suffices to say that the subject of lenses and filters warrants further investigation into these subjects at a different time. But the object of talking about lenses and filters in this chapter is to impress upon you how they affect our ability to respond or not respond to the technology of divine interception.

ARE YOU DRIVING

THROUGH A CLOUDY MIRROR?

Now we see things imperfectly as in a cloudy mirror, but then we will see everything with perfect clarity. All that I know now is partial and incomplete, but then I will know everything completely, just as God now knows me completely. 1 Corinthians 13:12

My wife will tell you that I do not like driving in bad weather, especially rainy and foggy weather. Whenever I have been intercepted by bad weather, I have quickly handed the reins of the car to my wife who is a better driver under these conditions. You might think I'm a coward but I am a man who was born in Africa, where we were blessed with endless sunshine. I'm convinced that driving in bad weather is not the will of God for His children. But anyone who has ever driven through stormy, rainy weather, especially foggy weather, knows that these types of conditions directly affect visibility while driving. These conditions greatly diminish a driver's capacity to control the car on the road. This is why most motor accidents happen during these adverse conditions.

While driving through foggy and rainy weather the windshield of any car usually becomes very cloudy. Visibility becomes greatly diminished in the process and driving becomes quite difficult. During these adverse weather conditions a driver's ability to respond to emergencies is also greatly diminished, especially at high speeds. In 1 Corinthians 13:12, the apostle Paul tells us that we are all driving through life while looking at clouded mirrors. Paul the Apostle says that we see through a glass darkly. It would seem to me that the apostle Paul is suggesting that we are all going through life with a set of lenses. Some of our lenses are much clearer than the lenses of others. But when we get to heaven we will see life with a greater sense of clarity.

Why is it important for us to heed the apostle Paul's warning? It is important for us to heed his warning lest we begin to trust in ourselves too much. We must accept with great humility that we do not know everything and that even our best perspective is distorted compared to God's perspective. It is this type of honesty with ourselves and humility before God that will set us up to become recipients of the technology of divine interception. Without humility we are going to miss many powerful moments of divine interception because we will trust what we are seeing through our clouded mirrors instead of what God is showing us at the time.

THE TRADITIONS OF MEN

Jesus replied, "And why do you, by your traditions, violate the direct commandments of God? Matthew 15:3

In my humble opinion, we need to take the warning found in Matthew 15:3 very seriously. In this verse Jesus identifies one of the most powerful filters that hinders many people on our planet from participating in the technology of divine interception. This particular filter is stopping many in His church from responding accurately to the technology of divine interception. This filter is called tradition. The Bible calls it the traditions of men.

> *A woman's relationship with her father establishes her identity, and how she FEELS about herself.*

Jesus rebuked the religious leaders of his day for allowing the traditions of men to violate the direct commandments of God. Said simply, Jesus was accusing them of allowing their traditions to shut down the operation of spiritual technology within the Kingdom of God. This passage shows us why many Kingdom citizens, who are bound to the traditions of their church, are going to miss many moments of divine interception – especially in situations where God releases the spirit of divine interception in a package that violates their long held traditions. I don't know about you but I refuse to miss divine interception because of the traditions of men. I want God to intercept me and demonic technologies that are headed toward me, but the traditions of men can never deliver me from this.

IS YOUR LUST MESSING YOU UP?

Let no man say when he is tempted, I am tempted of God: for God cannot be tempted with evil, neither tempteth he any man: [14]But every man is tempted, when he is drawn away of his own lust, and enticed. [15]Then when lust hath conceived, it bringeth forth sin: and sin, when it is finished, bringeth forth death. James 1:13-15

If you have been living in the Kingdom of God since the '80s, then you are probably aware of some of the sexual scandals that brought down the ministries of some prominent charismatic leaders in the body of Christ. Some of these mega-ministries were literally touching millions of

THE SPIRIT OF DIVINE INTERCEPTION

people around the world everyday. They commanded a huge following of loyal fans within the economy of the Kingdom.

Everything was going well for them until their ministry was mired in sexual scandal, and then everything fell apart. They had initiated the beginning of the end. For some of them the end started when the media discovered their secret indiscretions. In the wake of their fall from grace, they left a large company of disenfranchised fans and supporters who failed to understand what they perceived to be the hypocritical lifestyle of these ministers whom they had supported for a long time.

When great ministries that were touching millions of people disintegrate and then disappear into thin air, there are questions that come to mind. Questions such as: where was God in all of this? Why did God not intercept these men and women before they brought so much damage to the cause of Christ? My knowledge of God over the years has convinced me there is no scandal the body of Christ has ever experienced that God had not tried to intercept before the scandal became public. The interception failed because the person being intercepted refused to give up the demonic filter called "lust." By definition "lust" is desire which has become perverted because it has become disconnected from the purpose of God. Lust is the desire to gratify self at the expense of God and others. The apostle James also shows us that all temptation on the human level can be traced back to this filter called lust. Why is lust a filter instead of a lens? It is a filter because for the most part lust is governed by feelings more than logic. As a matter of fact, most extramarital affairs would never have happened if the feelings of the persons involved in the affair did not override their sanctified logic.

It is my heartfelt prayer that while you're reading this book that God would supernaturally intercept the engines of lust in your life before they destroy you and your testimony in God. It is my prayer that God would transform the engines of lust in your life into the engines of righteousness.

HOW IS YOUR PERCEPTION?

And it fell on a day, that Elisha passed to Shunem, where was a great woman; and she constrained him to eat bread. And so it

was, that as oft as he passed by, he turned in thither to eat bread.
⁹And she said unto her husband, Behold now, I perceive that this
is an holy man of God, which passeth by us continually. ¹⁰Let us
make a little chamber, I pray thee, on the wall; and let us set for
him there a bed, and a table, and a stool, and a candlestick: and
it shall be, when he cometh to us, that he shall turn in thither. 2
Kings 4:8-10

The final obstacle we are going to deal with that stops many people in our world from responding to the technology of divine interception is a very powerful lens called "perception." Perception is how we see things. It is how we view or treat other people. It is how we see and do business. Perception is like the rim around our reading glasses. It is in everything that we see and do. Perception is a very powerful lens that we cannot afford to ignore. It has serious ramifications on our ability to respond to whatever we are going through.

When Jesus was walking the earth he made it very clear that what people can receive from God is predicated upon their perception of who they thought He was. As the God-man incarnate Jesus could pretty much do anything, but he was limited by the perception of those around him. The Bible tells us that when Jesus went to hold a miracle service in his hometown of Nazareth he failed to do many mighty miracles because the people in his hometown failed to get over the fact that they knew him when he was growing up. They found it quite challenging to see him as the promised Messiah because it was much easier to see him as Mary's little boy. So the people of Nazareth missed their time of visitation because of their perception.

But the lens called "perception" also plays a critical role in our ability to respond to the technology of divine interception. For instance, when I was living in South Africa some years ago I discovered that white people considered it a taboo to receive anything from a black man. Historically white people were the business and land owners during the apartheid regime. So every black man or woman in search of a job had to go to a white person to get it. Over time white people in South Africa convinced themselves that receiving anything of value from a black man was a disgrace to their race.

Perception is how we see things. It is how we view or treat other people. It is how we see and do business.

When I moved to South Africa from Zambia, I was very naïve about the prevailing culture of this beautiful country. Before moving to South Africa the political ideology of "Apartheid" was lost on me. This is because I was born in a country where whites and blacks played and fellowshipped together. I had no idea what racial prejudice felt like until I got to South Africa where I was confronted with the perception that I was less than I thought I was because of the color of my skin.

I remember the time I stayed at a very large exotic hotel which was located in one of South Africa's premier national game parks. While I was staying at this exotic hotel God gave me a very powerful word of knowledge for a white South African couple that I'd never met before. But I knew that God was speaking to me about them. People who know me know that I have great boldness in doing the things God has anointed me to do. So, I went to this white couple and I gave them the word of the Lord.

Here is what God told me about them, *"Sir, the Holy Spirit has shown me that you just came from the doctor's office and the doctor told your wife that she will never be able to bear children. But God would have you know that He is going to give you a baby boy if you can receive the word of God's prophet and take it to heart!"* After I finished prophesying I could see that I had struck a nerve within this couple. The white man's wife began to weep profusely because I was so accurate. Going by the information I had given them, they had no doubt in their minds that God was speaking through me.

But without warning, the husband rushed his crying wife past me and refused my request for prayer. At first I was startled by his reaction and then I remembered that he was struggling with an inbuilt perception that had been grilled into him since he was a child. And the perception was, it is insulting and demeaning for white people to receive anything of value from a black man, even if what the black man was offering was prayer for a miracle. Since God had spoken to me about them with amazing accuracy, they did not go far before they chose to stop. When they stopped I heard the voice of the man calling for me. When I got to them he sheepishly asked me for prayer. When I looked at them they looked like African chickens that had been caught in the open by torrential rains. That is how uncomfortable the whole process was for them.

If I had not known any better, I would have thought I had them held at gunpoint. The embarrassment they were going through as I prayed for them was very surprising to me. It was then that I realized just how powerful the lens called perception really is. God was using me to supernaturally intercept a condition of barrenness in the life of this wife and the man was having a difficult time receiving from God because of his perception of me.

I know that if I had told him that all good things come packaged in black, he would have been devastated (just joking). So I did not mention that. I really believe that there are people who are missing great moments of divine interception because they have failed to perceive God in the people that He has sent to pray for them. This is why I've asked God to deliver me from every inbuilt perception that is not of God. I am determined to receive from God in whatever capacity He chooses to bless me in. I do not know who I am talking to at this juncture, but I know that somebody, somewhere, who is reading this book, is being intercepted at this exact moment. God is intercepting their perception of a man or a woman of God that He has placed in their life for their own deliverance.

LIFE APPLICATION SECTION

MEMORY VERSE

Now we see things imperfectly as in a cloudy mirror, but then we will see everything with perfect clarity. All that I know now is partial and incomplete, but then I will know everything completely, just as God now knows me completely. 1 Corinthians 13:12

REFLECTIONS

In you own words explain what L.E.N.S.es are?

_____

_____

_____

_____

_____

_____

In you own words explain what F.I.L.T.E.R.S. are?

_____

_____

_____

_____

_____

_____

JOURNAL YOUR THOUGHTS

CHAPTER FOUR
ABRAM SELLS HIS WIFE IN EGYPT

When Abram answered the call of God and left the land of his nativity for the Promised Land, he did not know that his choice to obey the voice of God had placed him on a collision course with one of the most powerful spiritual orders in all of creation. I have served God long enough to know that when we obey God and make choices that set us on course toward our God-given destiny, God will supernaturally weave himself into the matrix of our lives.

THE CALL

Now the LORD had said unto Abram, Get thee out of thy country, and from thy kindred, and from thy father's house, unto a land that I will shew thee: ²And I will make of thee a great nation, and I will bless thee, and make thy name great; and thou shalt be a blessing: ³And I will bless them that bless thee, and curse him that curseth thee: and in thee shall all families of the earth be blessed. Genesis 12:1-3 KJV

When God becomes involved with the affairs of our lives, the devil will also try to intercept the course of our lives to derail us from pursuing our spiritual destinies. The devil knows that from the moment the preceding word of God enters our air space, we enter into a season of spiritual transition until the word of the Lord concerning us has materialized. The devil knows that more often than not the negative impact of emotional upheaval, mental and financial stress combined with our human fragility, can force us to renegotiate our spiritual destiny.

Many of God's people abort and abdicate their Kingdom assignments during periods of such difficult transitions. Immediately after God gave Abram a powerful prophetic promise to migrate to the Promised Land, the devil tried to set him up for a fall using the vehicle of circumstance. Sometimes moments of difficult transition can leave us so disenfranchised or fearful that we are unable to cooperate with the technology of divine interception.

> *At that time a severe famine struck the land of Canaan, forcing Abram to go down to Egypt, where he lived as a foreigner.* [11] *As he was approaching the border of Egypt, Abram said to his wife, Sarai, "Look, you are a very beautiful woman.* [12] *When the Egyptians see you, they will say, 'This is his wife. Let's kill him; then we can have her!'* [13] *So please tell them you are my sister. Then they will spare my life and treat me well because of their interest in you." Genesis 12:10-13*

Without any obvious warning, demonic agencies from the second heaven (the devil's headquarters) began to manipulate the spiritual atmosphere and natural climate around Abram's habitat. These demonic powers stopped the chambers of the first heaven from pouring rain on the land Abram was living on! This resulted in a serious famine which dried up every well and water source around Abram. The ensuing drought caused Abram to panic and forced him to reconsider his God-given position. Abram made a hasty decision out of his own sense of panic and insecurity and headed to the godless nation of Egypt. *This decision would haunt Abram for a very long time.*

When we know there is a high calling of God upon our lives, we must train ourselves to run to God during times of painful transition.

If we fail to do so, we will make hasty decisions which will serve to strengthen the demonic technology and agenda against us. Abram made a hasty decision and ran to Egypt because he was not firmly grounded in his relationship with God. Abram did not know the awesome power of the spiritual order that he had been called to serve under. Abram's behavior in crisis mirrors the experiences of many Kingdom citizens who are not deeply rooted in their knowledge of God.

> *And sure enough, when Abram arrived in Egypt, everyone spoke of Sarai's beauty. [15] When the palace officials saw her, they sang her praises to Pharaoh, their king, and Sarai was taken into his palace. [16] Then Pharaoh gave Abram many gifts because of her— sheep, goats, cattle, male and female donkeys, male and female servants, and camels. [17] But the LORD sent terrible plagues upon Pharaoh and his household because of Sarai, Abram's wife. Genesis 12:14-17*

BROKEN COVENANTS

When Abram and his household approached the borders of Egypt, Abram turned to his wife Sarai and had a conversation with her that would be every married woman's nightmare. Instead of risking his life for her, Abram asked his wife to lie about the true nature of their relationship. Abram was afraid of the Egyptians discovering that he was the husband of such a beautiful woman and he believed they would kill him so they could present her to Pharaoh. Sarai, being a submissive wife, agreed with Abram's flawed proposal and the covenant of marriage between them was broken!

> *Abram's behavior in crisis mirrors the experiences of many Kingdom citizens who are not deeply rooted in their knowledge of God.*

Covenants are made and broken with words. This is why our words are very important and carry great weight in the spirit realm. When demonic agencies saw that the spiritual boundaries around Abram's marriage had been breached, evil spirits rushed in like a pack of African hyenas to the slaughter. Pharaoh's officers wasted no time telling their lustful king that a beautiful Hebrew woman had just come into the land of Egypt. This is why Kingdom entrepreneurs who do not know how to trust God in times of crisis in their vehicle of commerce can be easily seduced by demonic powers. It is easy to be compromised when we are already compromised. Like Abram, many Kingdom businessmen and women are misrepresenting God in the marketplace.

The king of Egypt wasted no time bringing Sarai into his bedroom. In exchange for anticipated sexual escapades with Sarai, Pharaoh treated Abram with great kindness because he thought Abram was Sarai's brother. The king of Egypt gave Abram a great company of sheep, oxen, camels and donkeys. He also gave Abram many male and female servants. Abram became a rich man overnight by lying and selling his wife to a demonic system. Kingdom businessmen and women must be careful that they do not adopt deceptive business practices which guarantee quick profits but violate principles of common decency and integrity. This is why all Kingdom citizens, especially Kingdom entrepreneurs, need to be introduced to the technology of divine interception.

I can imagine that Abram was horrified by the prospect of having his wife raped by a lustful Egyptian king. Using Sarai as a sexual toy was definitely what the king of Egypt had in mind when he brought her into his bedroom. Fortunately, God intervened and terrorized the house of Pharaoh with grievous plagues. God warned Pharaoh against sexually exploiting Sarai because she was the wife of a prophet of God. Pharaoh quickly restored her to her husband and instructed his servants to drive Abram and his household out of the land of Egypt.

So Pharaoh summoned Abram and accused him sharply. "What have you done to me?" he demanded. "Why didn't you tell me she was your wife? [19] Why did you say, 'She is my sister,' and allow me to take her as my wife? Now then, here is your wife. Take her and get out of here!" [20] Pharaoh ordered some of his men to escort them, and he sent Abram out of the country, along with his wife and all his possessions. Genesis 12:18-20

Abram's testimony of compromise that was manifested in Egypt is one of the reasons why many unbelievers do not believe that many men and women of God are for real. I cannot blame unbelievers who have lost confidence in the global church's leadership because of the many scandals that have mushroomed within the leadership of the global church. But do not lose hope my friend; there is a spiritual technology from heaven that is going to intercept many of these scandals that have brought shame to the name of Christ before they actually take place.

MIXED BLESSINGS

When Abram and Sarai left Egypt they had more material possessions than they had come with. The king of Egypt had given them a generous bounty before he realized that Abram had deceived him. When Pharaoh threw them out of the country he refused to take back the riches that he had given to Abram in exchange for Sarai. But the possessions that the king of Egypt gave to Abram turned out to be more of a *"curse than a blessing."* It is regrettable when unbelievers have more integrity than the so-called Kingdom businessmen and women. This is definitely a freak of nature; things are not supposed to be this way.

The blessing of the LORD makes a person rich, and he adds no sorrow with it. Proverbs 10:22

When the spiritual technology of how we raise money in our church or business is not accurate, we will release what I call *"mixed blessings"* into our lives. *A mixed blessing by definition is a blessing that is mingled with a demonic principle.* Abram's Ishmael is an example of a mixed blessing. *The biggest problem with mixed blessings is that they always create more pain than the pleasure they promise.* Mixed blessings will always place undue burdens upon our future destiny. Mixed blessings always attack the future, while doing very little for us in the present. Perhaps this is the reason why the devil does not want many Kingdom businessmen and women to allow the Holy Spirit to inspect the technology of how they galvanize their resources. Satan wants God's people to take shortcuts within the economy of the Kingdom. The devil wants Kingdom citizens to short-circuit the future by buying into a half-baked blessing in the present.

> *Covenants are made and broken with words. This is why our words are very important and carry great weight in the spirit realm.*

There is a reason why demonic powers are wrecking havoc in the lives of so many Kingdom entrepreneurs. *The Bible says that the causeless curse shall not arise.* So why is it that many Kingdom businessmen and women are losing their families and marriages to demonic powers the more they prosper financially? I believe that it is because there is an open door that is allowing demonic powers to come through because the technology they're using for raising money is not accurate before God. If God does not intercept many of the inaccurate methods that most Kingdom entrepreneurs are using to raise resources, demonic powers will continue to terrorize the people of God. I am trusting God to use this writing to intercept many inaccurate patterns of raising finances in the lives of His people. It is my prayer that God would use this book to teach us the *"ways of the Spirit."*

PROPHETIC PARELLELS

In the Scriptures there are many prophetic symbols, shadows and types. Women in Scripture are a prophetic representation of the church or a business entity. Women are also prophetic symbols of an entity, which has the power to multiply what is sown into it. *Said simply, women represent the power of multiplication.* In marriage for instance, the man may inject his sperm into the woman's womb but when the woman gives back what the man planted inside her, she gives back something much larger than what was deposited in her.

For the sake of our study in this particular book we will say that Sarai as a woman represents the following things prophetically:

- Sarai in our story represents the church (body of Christ)

- Sarai represents the power of multiplication

- Sarai also represents a Kingdom business

- Abram in our story represents the leader or spiritual covering over a Kingdom entity

These three prophetic representations clearly show us why the devil and God are both fighting for control of your "prophetic Sarai." What Abram did to Sarai in Egypt when he sold her to a demonic system in order to preserve himself is still happening today. Many leaders in the body of Christ are manipulating or prostituting their churches in order to advance themselves financially. I know of pastors who bring into their churches very manipulative speakers for the purpose of raising vast sums of money from their already financially strapped church members in order to fatten the pastor's wallet. These special speakers or fundraisers are usually called "hired guns." They normally use prophecy as a vehicle of manipulating gullible saints into giving more money than they can possibly afford. This is an abomination before God and the spirit of divine interception is going to destroy and intercept this foolishness within His church.

Sarai also represents Kingdom businesses that are being sold out to the systems of this world by Kingdom entrepreneurs who are already compromised. There are far too many so-called Christian businessmen and women who are building business empires for the express purpose of competing with the "Jones's" than for the purpose of glorifying God. In the parable of the talents the Lord Jesus made it very clear that those who are called to the *"Mountain of Business"* within the economy of the Kingdom are going to account for what they did with the business that God gave them for Kingdom advancement. If you are a Kingdom businessman or woman and this book has landed in your lap, I want to challenge you not to sell out your Kingdom business to the king of Egypt just because you want to survive the recession. Your business that God gave you is your Sarai. Do not allow the king of Egypt to sleep with your Sarai (business) because God has invested your future in your Sarai (business).

PROSPERING THROUGH DECEPTION

One of the main things the Holy Spirit wants to intercept among Kingdom citizens is the *"principle of prospering through deception."* Just because something works does not mean it's right. When a prostitute enters the red light district and men begin to contract her for sex and she ends up making a lot of money, that does not make her profession right. God is very interested in the *"roots and origins of the prosperity of His people."* There are just too many crooked and untrustworthy so-called Christian businessmen and women. It is quite regrettable when I'm told by many Kingdom businessmen and women that they are terrified of doing business with their fellow brothers and sisters in Christ. I've been told by many of the Josephs and Daniels that I am mentoring that they have lost more money dealing with Christians in business than they have in doing business with the world. This demonic reproach on the church must come to an end. Kingdom citizens *"prospering through deception are one of the primary targets of the technology of divine interception that God is initiating within his church globally."*

\

LIFE APPLICATION SECTION

MEMORY VERSE

At that time a severe famine struck the land of Canaan, forcing Abram to go down to Egypt, where he lived as a foreigner. [11] As he was approaching the border of Egypt, Abram said to his wife, Sarai, "Look, you are a very beautiful woman. [12] When the Egyptians see you, they will say, 'This is his wife. Let's kill him; then we can have her!' [13] So please tell them you are my sister. Then they will spare my life and treat me well because of their interest in you."

Genesis 12:10-13

REFLECTIONS

Why did Abram sell his wife in Egypt?

_____

_____

_____

_____

_____

_____

How did this action open a door for demonic powers in Abram's future destiny?

_____

_____

_____

_____

_____

_____

ABRAM SELLS HIS WIFE IN EGYPT

JOURNAL YOUR THOUGHTS

_____
_____
_____
_____
_____
_____
_____
_____
_____
_____
_____
_____
_____
_____
_____
_____
_____
_____
_____
_____
_____
_____
_____
_____
_____
_____
_____
_____
_____
_____

CHAPTER FIVE
SNAKES IN MONEY BAGS

During the course of writing my first book, titled *The Order of Melchizedek*, God gave me a revelation that shook me to the core of my being. This is what the Holy Spirit told me: *"Son, for as long as the church thinks that Genesis 13:1-2 is an example of supernatural prosperity, it is never going to experience real Kingdom wealth."* This statement shook me to the core of my being because I have used Genesis 13:1-2 many times in my teachings on Kingdom prosperity. The Holy Spirit continued, *"Son, Genesis 13:1-2 is not the basis for real Kingdom wealth because Genesis 13:1-2 describes Abram's tainted wealth that he obtained by selling his wife to a demonic system."* The Holy Spirit told me that tainted wealth can never form the basis of real Kingdom wealth. The Holy Spirit then said something to me that put the icing on the cake, *"Many preachers and businessmen in the body of Christ are doing the same thing that Abram did to his wife while he was in Egypt. They are prostituting the body of Christ or their business for money and then calling their resulting prosperity real Kingdom wealth."* When the Holy Spirit said this to me I had to repent because I discovered that I was also "found wanting."

So Abram left Egypt and traveled north into the Negev, along with his wife and Lot and all that they owned. [2] (Abram was very rich in livestock, silver, and gold.) Genesis 13:1-2

THE METHOD COUNTS

God is interested in how his people acquire resources. The spiritual technology that God's people use to raise money can either unleash the blessing of God or demonic powers. Jesus already told us in the Gospels that money (unrighteous mammon) is found in abundance in the realms of unrighteousness. This is why a prostitute or a seductress can put on a very enticing outfit and then walk the streets looking for men willing to pay for sex. Within a couple of hours of selling her body to the highest bidder, she will make more money in those few hours of sin than most people do in a week working at a decent job. This is why having a lot of money does not mean that we are living under the favor of His presence. I really believe that the more gold we acquire the more we need God. Inaccurate patterns of raising money can open up a demonic portal for the devil to attack us even though we are citizens of the Kingdom of God. This book, among other things, will seek to intercept inaccurate patterns of raising money that have given the devil the license to attack many church leaders and marketplace ministers within the economy of the Kingdom.

Lot, who was traveling with Abram, had also become very wealthy with flocks of sheep and goats, herds of cattle, and many tents. [6] But the land could not support both Abram and Lot with all their flocks and herds living so close together. [7] So disputes broke out between the herdsmen of Abram and Lot. (At that time Canaanites and Perizzites were also living in the land.)[8] Finally Abram said to Lot, "Let's not allow this conflict to come between us or our herdsmen. After all, we are close relatives! [9] The whole countryside is open to you. Take your choice of any section of the land you want, and we will separate. If you want the land to the left, then I'll take the land on the right. If you prefer the land on the right, then I'll go to the left."[10] Lot took a long look at the *fertile plains of the Jordan Valley in the direction of Zoar. The whole area was well watered everywhere, like the garden of the LORD or the beautiful land of Egypt. (This was before the LORD destroyed Sodom and Gomorrah.) ¹¹ Lot chose for himself the whole Jordan Valley to the east of them. He went there with his flocks and servants and parted company with his uncle Abram. ¹² So Abram settled in the land of Canaan, and Lot moved his tents to a place near Sodom and settled among the cities of the plain. ¹³ But the people of this area were extremely wicked and constantly sinned against the LORD. Genesis 13:8-13*

The Holy Spirit told me that tainted wealth can never form the basis of real Kingdom wealth.

Immediately after Abram returned from the land of Egypt, serious in-fighting broke out between Abram's herdsmen and those of Lot. The demonic snakes that were buried in the money bags they had taken from the king of Egypt were already beginning to manifest themselves in the form of strife and division in Abram's house! The only thing that saved the day was Abram's attitude of humility and his ability to choose the high road. The memory of how God's power had rescued his wife from the jaws of a dangerous demonic system in the land of Egypt had left an indelible mark on Abram's impressionable spirit. Abram was slowly beginning to understand the power of the spiritual order that he had brought himself under when he answered the call of God.

Instead of fighting with Lot, Abram told his nephew that they needed to separate. Furthermore Abram told Lot that he was free to choose whatever land space he needed to sustain his livestock. Abram chose to take whatever was left over. Lot, who was already infected by the spirit of the king of Egypt, chose the rich portion of land which was next to Sodom. Sodom was the most wicked nation of the ancient world. Sodom was also the birthplace of every form of sexual perversion, including homosexuality. Lot's carnal decision set the stage for the chain of events that would soon set Abram on a collision course with the king of Sodom and the priestly Order of Melchizedek.

THE DEVIL WANTS THE SECOND GENERATION

The spiritual ramifications of Abram's business decision to sell out his wife to a demonic system in order to serve his company in a time of global economic recession were deep and far-reaching. The most serious ramification took place in his nephew's heart. I'm sure that Lot looked up to his uncle who had adopted him after the sudden demise of his father, Haran. I am sure that Lot had listened to Abram recount the story of how God called him out of Babylon to inherit the Promised Land. Lot heard his uncle talk about his faith in a big God, but failed to live by it when his business was threatened with financial collapse. I can almost see the look of dismay and confusion that must have plastered his face when the Egyptian guards came to escort his auntie to Pharaoh's palace after his uncle sold her off! I really believe it was at this point that Lot's respect for Abram as a man of God diminished.

By the time Abram and Lot got back to the Land of Promise the damage had already been done. Abram's sleazy business decision in the marketplace had activated the process of spiritual decline in Lot's life. In this story Lot represents many of today's disillusioned sons and daughters who have become weary of the institution of Church because they watch their parents play church on Sunday and then they see how their parents misrepresent God in the marketplace. This is why God is determined to intercept the means and methods that Kingdom citizens use to unlock financial resources. This is the area that is destroying the second generation while opening doors for demonic powers to infiltrate the apostolic community of believers. I am so tired of seeing Kingdom entrepreneurs lose their wives and children the richer they get. Something is seriously wrong with this picture. May the good Lord unleash His supernatural interception technology and place an end to this madness within His Church!

Abram's sleazy business decision in the marketplace had activated the process of spiritual decline in Lot's life.

LOT MOVES TO SODOM

Abram's decision to move to Egypt during the time of famine (economic recession) muddied his relationship with his nephew, Lot. Whenever we disobey God in our decision-making process, the spiritual consequences of our spiritual inaccuracy almost always manifests in the arena of our closest personal or business relationships. This was certainly the case between Abram and Lot. As soon as they returned from Egypt with the bounty taken from the treasuries of Egypt, there was serious strife and division between their two corporations. The presence of spirits of strife and division in our closest relationships is always a sign that demonic agencies are swimming in the "spiritual wells" we are drinking from.

The strife between Abram's and Lot's herdsmen quickly became hostile. Abram called for a truce. Abram told Lot that there was no need for them to fight over land (business contracts) because they were family. *Kingdom businessmen and women must never fight each other over "filthy lucre," because there are no shortages of resources in the economy of the Kingdom.* Even though Abram had seniority, he gave Lot the power of first choice concerning the land. (Coincidentally, when we come into a place of spiritual maturity, we can do more with the "leftovers" than most people can do with a whole pie.) The intervention of God that Abram had just experienced in the land of Egypt was still fresh on his mind. He remembered how God had delivered his wife from Pharaoh's bedchamber and spared his own life. This powerful intervention of God had left an indelible mark on Abram's spirit. He was beginning to appreciate the power of the God who had called him out of Babylon. This is why he refused to fight with Lot over the issue of land. On the other hand, Lot did not know how to make spiritual decisions from his spirit-man. *Kingdom businessmen and women who master the art of listening to the Lord before making major business decisions, will never ever lose money in any business deal.*

INTERCEPTING THE REPROACH OF EGYPT

Abram replied to the king of Sodom, "I solemnly swear to the Lord, God Most High, Creator of heaven and earth that I will not take so much as a single thread or sandal thong from what belongs to you. Otherwise you might say, 'I am the one who made Abram rich." Genesis 14:22-3

After Abram and Sarai left Egypt with an abundance of material possessions that Abram had obtained by deceiving the king of Egypt, then the king of Egypt told everyone who had an ear to listen that he was the one who had made Abram rich. These malicious rumors followed Abram wherever he went. It was quite embarrassing to say the least. *When Abram met Melchizedek (the priest of God Most High) he received a revelation of how he could sanctify his tainted wealth.* Abram gave Melchizedek a tithe of all he had. *This divinely inspired tithe not only destroyed the spirit of greed in Abram's life, it also became the supernatural purifying element which sanctified everything that Abram owned!* Abram's tithes into this eternal King-Priest brought everything that he owned into divine alignment. Abram's tithes into the Order of Melchizedek rolled away the reproach of Egypt from his life. This is why it is so important for the global Church to rediscover the Abrahamic tithing model. In a later chapter I will go into greater detail explaining why "tithing" is one of the most powerful prerequisites for manifesting the technology of divine interception in our life or vehicle of commerce.

When the king of Sodom offered Abram gold and silver from the treasuries of Sodom, Abram knew that he could not afford to make the same mistake twice. Abram knew that if he took the money, the king of Sodom was going to join the king of Egypt in declaring that he was the one who had made Abram rich. Abram's refusal of the king of Sodom's generous offer underscores the *power of tithing* into the Order of Melchizedek.

In many parts of the world the Church is not trusted by many in the world who have observed the fact that there are as many financial scandals in the Church as they see in the secular world. This has left a very deep and far reaching reproach on the body of Christ worldwide. By definition a "reproach" is an object of scorn or contempt. In many parts and social circles of the world the Church is truly an "object of scorn and contempt." But God is supernaturally intercepting and overturning the reproach of the world off His covenant people, especially many of those who are giving up the "seducing influences of the Christian religion" to embrace the "Unshakable Kingdom." This powerful interception technology that Heaven is releasing over citizens of the Kingdom all over the world shall bring the Church into a place of great favor and prominence like Joseph and Daniel of old.

SAYING NO TO THE KING OF SODOM

After Abram returned from his victory over Kedorlaomer and all his allies, the king of Sodom went out to meet him in the valley of Shaveh (that is, the King's Valley). Genesis 14:17

While Abram was returning from the slaughter of the kings from the East, news of his glorious victory reached the ears of the king of Sodom. The king of Sodom drove his royal chariot to intercept Abram on his victorious return. The "king of Sodom" represents a demonic system that wants to ensnare Kingdom businessmen and women in the marketplace. Abram did not know that the king of Sodom was riding ferociously toward him, but the Lord did. The setting and timing God chose to introduce Abram to the priestly Order of Melchizedek is very significant indeed. The perfect spiritual timing of Melchizedek's appearance in Abram's life will shed light on the awesome power that this eternal priestly order possesses. It was no coincidence that God in His infinite wisdom chose to intercept Abram's life just before the king of Sodom reached him. God was determined to touch Abram before the devil's greatest agent did.

> *The "king of Sodom" represents a demonic system that wants to ensnare Kingdom businessmen and women in the marketplace.*

PRE-EMPTIVE WARFARE

Many spiritual leaders have asked me to define what I mean by the phrase "divine interception." Here is the definition that the Lord gave me. He said "divine interception" means that "God gets to you first and then takes you in, before the devil has had a chance to 'take you out!'" *This definition means that the "technology of divine interception" operates within the parameters of "pre-emptive warfare."* "Pre-emptive warfare" is the most advanced and bloodless form of warfare. This type of warfare has a "zero casualty" ratio on the side of the nation initiating the pre-emptive strike. Even though this type of warfare has zero casualties on the part of the nation initiating such an attack, it is the most lethal form of warfare on enemy combatants because the enemy is almost always caught by surprise. This book is about the supernatural restoration of this type of warfare within His church to help minimize the number of Kingdom citizens who fall prey to the wicked one. Restoring this type of "zero casualty" warfare is what the technology of divine interception is all about.

> *The king of Sodom said to Abram, "Give back my people who were captured. But you may keep for yourself all the goods you have recovered." Abram replied to the king of Sodom, "I solemnly swear to the Lord, God Most High, Creator of heaven and earth, that I will not take so much as a single thread or sandal thong from what belongs to you. Otherwise you might say, 'I am the one who made Abram rich.' Genesis 14:21-23*

Remember that Sodom was more wicked than any of the countries of the East. Sodom made Egypt look like it was a paradise of righteousness. Please bear in mind that the Egyptians were no saints; they were hardcore idol worshippers. They worshipped Pharaoh, frogs, lice, the sun, and the river Nile just to name a few, and yet the people of Sodom made the Egyptians look like saints. The people of Sodom were ultra social liberals who did not believe in any kind of divine or moral restraint.

This was the same king whose royal chariots were charging ferociously toward Abram who was headed toward the Valley of Shaveh. The Valley of Shaveh is also known as the King's Valley, because it became the showdown stage for the confrontation between two kings from two different kingdoms. The divine confrontation was between the king of Sodom, who was the personification of the devil, and Melchizedek, king of Jerusalem and Priest of God Most High who represented the Kingdom of God.

"Divine interception" means that "God gets to you first and then takes you in, before the devil has had a chance to 'take you out!'"

When the king of Sodom finally reached Abram, he was a moment too late. The king of Jerusalem and High Priest of God Most High had already intercepted Abram, and Abram had been fully introduced to the priestly Order of Melchizedek. Abram had already partaken of the bread and wine of this heavenly Order and had been changed from the inside out. There was a divine power working inside his spirit and mind like he had never known before. When the king of Sodom tried to bribe him, Abram refused his luring offer. Abram told the king that he had nothing that Abram desired, even down to the shoelaces of the people of Sodom whom he had rescued. Abram's obedience coupled with his encounter with the priestly Order of Melchizedek gave him the power to rise above the seductive power and influence of the king of Sodom. In doing so, Abram side-stepped the demonic agencies connected to the king of Sodom.

Abram's encounter with Melchizedek's priesthood gave him the supernatural power to resist every demonic entity that was coming against him through the king of Sodom. This divine encounter also gave Abram the power to say "NO" to a very lucrative business proposal that the king of Sodom presented him, which was worth multiple millions of dollars. I have seen too many good ministers and businessmen who have been destroyed like flies because they failed to say "NO" to the seductive influence of the king of Sodom (symbolic of Satan and this world system).

SATAN'S ISHMAEL VERSUS GOD'S ISAAC

God had made a covenant promise to Abram that he would give him a son who would be born through Sarai. When God first gave this prophetic promise to Abram and Sarai it was much easier for them to believe it. They were both relatively young. Then months turned into many years of waiting. *Along the way Sarai herself gave up the hope of becoming a mother in her old age, so she devised a plan that was in actuality the kiss of death.* Sarai decided to help God fulfill His word of promise by telling Abram to sleep with her Egyptian maid Hagar so that the child she would bear would be Sarai's.

> *It did not take much time to make my decision. God allowed the devil to overplay his hand to show me the dangerous position I was in, in the realm of the Spirit.*

I imagine that Sarai did not have a difficult time selling her new idea to her aging husband. How often does an old married man get the blessing of his wife to sleep with a beautiful eighteen-year-old maid? Abram was probably in Hagar's tent long before Sarai could have second thoughts. From the outside, Sarai's plan looked brilliant. But she and Abram had walked into a demonic trap. They made a monumental error that would haunt them for the rest of their lives.

So Abram had sexual relations with Hagar, and she became pregnant. But when Hagar knew she was pregnant, she began to treat her mistress, Sarai, with contempt. Then Sarai said to Abram, "This is all your fault! I put my servant into your arms, but now that she's pregnant she treats me with contempt. The Lord will show who's wrong—you or me!" Genesis 16:4-5

Like a rattlesnake that has been forced into a corner, Sarai's brilliant plan quickly backfired and struck at the core of her marriage with Abram. The son born through her Egyptian maid whom she had thought would bring her great joy only brought sorrow and death into her life. The ensuing spiritual tension caused Abram and Sarai to begin to have marital problems. The true roots and origins of what they had created were paving a way for the devil to attack them.

Sarai wondered why her sincere and well-thought-out plan to help God turned so terribly wrong. The answer is found in understanding spiritual roots and origins. If something has its roots and origins in a satanic power play, there is little we can do to change the true nature of what the thing really is. *Hagar's son, Ishmael, was born out of a spirit of self-will and rebellion to God's authority.* There was no way this child could bring the fullness of joy and laughter which God had promised would come with the birth of Isaac. The spiritual roots and origins of Abram's Ishmael went all the way back to the ten gods of Egypt, not to mention the devil himself who was the principal spirit behind Egyptian idolatry.

When the appointed time came for God's Isaac to be born, Abram had a difficult time releasing his faith because he was so enamored with the child that he had produced by his own power. Abram actually interceded for Ishmael. He asked God to have Ishmael replace Isaac. God would not hear of it. God refused to hear of it because Abram did not know the spiritual ramifications of what he was asking. *He did not know that when something is built on demonic technology, its root system is embedded in hellish operations.* No matter what God did to Ishmael, Ishmael would have remained at best half divine and half devilish. "Ishmael was a mixed blessing." Said plainly "Ishmael" was the "price" that the devil had set on Abram's future destiny because of the "money" that Abram had taken deceptively from the hands of the king of Egypt. There are many church and marketplace leaders who are paying a heavy price because of the "Ishmaels" that their inaccurate business dealings have produced. Their past business dealings have now mortgaged their "future destiny" in the Kingdom.

TAINTED AND DEFILED OFFERINGS

But there was a certain man named Ananias who, with his wife, Sapphira, sold some property. ² He brought part of the money to the apostles, claiming it was the full amount. With his wife's consent, he kept the rest.³ Then Peter said, "Ananias, why have you let Satan fill your heart? You lied to the Holy Spirit, and you kept some of the money for yourself. ⁴ The property was yours to sell or not sell, as you wished. And after selling it, the money was also yours to give away. How could you do a thing like this? You weren't lying to us but to God!"⁵ As soon as Ananias heard these words, he fell to the floor and died. Everyone who heard about it was terrified. ⁶ Then some young men got up, wrapped him in a sheet, and took him out and buried him. Acts 5:1-6

Seriously speaking, some of the methods that citizens of the Kingdom are using to "unlock financial resources" are bringing the angel of death and the technology of death into the life stream of the Church. In the Western world most particularly, our concept of revival is of a God who comes to simply baptize us with fire. Very few of us in the West have been to God ordained revivals where people drop dead in the Church while God is moving in His holiness. How many of us would go to a church where people dropped dead for "lying and giving tainted offerings?" This is exactly what happened when Ananias and his wife Sapphira came through the doors of the apostolic church, which was at Jerusalem.

This couple had entered into a demonic alliance to lie to God's apostles by concealing the actual sales price of their property which they had dedicated to God. So they collectively entered the temple of God with a demonic technology operating within their souls. Said in another way, by the time they both stepped through the doors of the Church their offerings were already defiled. But unfortunately for them Peter the Apostle was a sure vehicle of the most powerful spiritual technology in creation for effecting pre-emptive warfare: the technology of divine interception.

God, working through Peter, intercepted the demonic agenda which was hell bent on contaminating the apostolic community and undermining the apostolic revival. There are many present day couples like "Ananias and Sapphira" in the global church who are contaminating the streams of the apostolic revival in His Church because of "tithing or giving" into the church monies obtained by using demonic technology and principles. God is about to supernaturally intercept these tainted and defiled offerings in His Church.

IS YOUR GIFT MEASURED IN DOLLAR$

When Simon saw that the Spirit was given when the apostles laid their hands on people, he offered them money to buy this power. [19] "Let me have this power, too," he exclaimed, "so that when I lay my hands on people, they will receive the Holy Spirit!"[20] But Peter replied, "May your money be destroyed with you for thinking God's gift can be bought! [21] You can have no part in this, for your heart is not right with God. [22] Repent of your wickedness and pray to the Lord. Perhaps he will forgive your evil thoughts, [23] for I can see that you are full of bitter jealousy and are held captive by sin."[24] "Pray to the Lord for me," Simon exclaimed, "that these terrible things you've said won't happen to me!" Acts 8:18-24

This final passage of this chapter, "snakes in money bags" was the most difficult for me to write because it directly impacts those whom I love and honor deeply. It affects stationary and itinerant ministers of the gospel. This passage was difficult for me to write because I am also a five-fold minister of the glorious gospel. I am the senior pastor of a thriving church, but I am also an itinerant minister. It was also difficult because I do not want to seem like I am empowering the rebellious in the Church to dishonor God's anointed servants. But I am more afraid of disobeying God and contaminating my apostolic call to the greater body of Christ than I am of being misunderstood.

> *I am more afraid of disobeying God and contaminating my apostolic call to the greater body of Christ than I am of being misunderstood.*

I am an apostolic reformer by calling and I find it difficult masking the truth when it is calling to be told without fear or compromise. Many people in the Church are looking for reformation in His temple. The only problem with the spirit of reformation is that it will cause us to look under the carpet to see things we swept under when we were not ready to face the truth. But what God wants to intercept in this final passage is very critical to both the future and wellbeing of the greater body of Christ.

Here we go…! God told me that He is about to supernaturally "intercept" the "spirit of Simon the sorcerer" that has infected many of His spiritual leaders in the Body of Christ. The spirit of Simon the sorcerer is the spirit that feels like it can "attach a monetary value" to the gift of God. When Philip the evangelist went into the city of Samaria God used him mightily with undeniable signs and wonders. There was a notable sorcerer in the city by the name of Simon who had terrorized the people of Samaria with his sorcery. But when he saw the power of God in demonstration through Philip's ministry he gave his life to Christ.

But it was not until the arrival of the apostles that Simon's level of conversion was put to the test. When the apostles came to Samaria to assist Philip in this city-taking mission, they began to lay hands on people to receive the baptism in the Holy Ghost. When Simon the sorcerer saw that through the laying on of hands by the apostles the Holy Spirit was imparted to people and they began to speak in other tongues, he was overly impressed. Simon was so moved by how God was using the apostles that he offered them a lot of money in exchange for the power to impart the Holy Spirit to others. Peter the Apostle rebuked him harshly for thinking that the gift of God could be purchased with money. To Simon's credit, he repented quickly and asked Peter the Apostle to pray for his deliverance.

God told me that He is very grieved by the degree that the spirit of Simon the sorcerer has infiltrated the lives of so many of His anointed servants. God told me that *"If a man's gift is measured in dollars and cents instead of his obedience to God, the process of spiritual and moral decline"* has already started. In today's Church there are many anointed servants of God who will not move a finger to go and preach anywhere unless the "money is right!" They live by this demonic philosophy "if the money is right then God must be sending them." What is even more regrettable is that ministers who number themselves among God's "apostles and prophets" have also joined the pack. Since apostles and prophets are two foundational ministries of the New Testament church, the "cracks" in the foundation of His temple have only become bigger. But God will have the last say. Many of His servants are getting ready to go through a major interception in this arena.

There are many great and famous men and women of God who can be "bought into a speaking engagement" provided the money is right. I am reminded of the popular TV show, *The Price is Right*. For many years a lot of us watched the legendary TV icon Bob Barker call contestants to the floor by telling them "come on down!" Many anointed servants of God will "come on down" for as long as you can name or afford their price. This is because their gift is not measured in "obedience to God;" it's measured in "dollars and cents." What a tragedy. I wonder how many witches and warlocks have walked through the doors of the Church and bought up many anointed servants of God like houses in foreclosure.

> *"If a man's gift is measured in dollars and cents instead of his obedience to God, the process of spiritual and moral decline" has already started.*

I am not suggesting that hosting ministries must NOT take care of God's servants. Many of my speakers know that I am a very generous man and host - a badge that my wife and I love to wear proudly. I know the struggles that many pastors go through, so when they come to my church I want to be a great blessing to them. But this does not give pastors and other five-fold ministers the license to "prostitute" the Body of Christ in order to advance themselves. Host ministries who steal from visiting speakers are also courting a "curse" for a "causeless curse shall not arise," the Bible declares. I know that there are important and reasonable financial considerations to think about when accepting speaking engagements, which can be addressed within reason. However the unchecked greed of some ministers is placing the Church under ransom and I promise you, God said that the "day of Interception for many ministers, who are misrepresenting Christ in this arena, has come."

GOD SAID SOW $7777

A dear pastor friend of mine in the Bahamas went through a very embarrassing ordeal that no Pastor should ever have to go through in front of his entire congregation. He invited a prophet to speak at his church on a Sunday morning, but the prophet turned out to be a "prophet-liar." According to my friend this prophet had an amazing word of knowledge and prophetic ministry that was razor sharp. He was so accurate that he would tell some of his members what kind of cars they drove.

My friend told me that his Church was beaming with unfeigned excitement at the prophet's powerful ministry. My friend felt proud of himself that he had scheduled such an incredible speaker and prophetic gift. But his joy was very short-lived. The problems started to surface when the prophet began to take up the love offering from the people in His church. My friend told me that it was like giving with a gun pointed to your head, except in this case the gun was a "prophecy gun." But things were about to get worse.

The prophet called my friend to the pulpit and asked him to face his congregation which he did, graciously. Then came the bomb shell. "Pastor, God says that in order for you to seal the breakthrough that God has given your people this morning, you must sow a special prophetic seed of $7777 into my life." My friend told me that he felt like a deer caught in the headlights of a car. He was deeply embarrassed by the ordeal and so was his wife who sat in the front pews of the church. His daughters who were in service were very upset, because they knew that their father did not have $7777 anywhere.

His teenage daughters were spiritual enough to know that if anybody knew their father did not have $7777, it was the Lord. My friend told me that at the time he only had $2000 to his name and yet this false prophet was asking him to give $7777 in front of his congregation. He told me that in order to protect the shaky faith of baby believers in his Church, he wrote a check to the false prophet for the amount. He wrote a check he knew would be cancelled as soon as service was over. He told me that in twenty-five years of leading his congregation he had never lied to them until then. My question is, "what happened to us? How did we get so messed up? What makes us think that a God who owns everything would force His people to give beyond their means and grudgingly so? Why is it that Old Testament prophets sometimes refused to accept large offerings from people they were ministering to, but we accept every "offering" from anybody, even when their motivation for giving is dubious?"

I am not asking these questions to cast a bad light on servants of the gospel because I am one of them. The truth of the matter is that in every generation God always has a righteous remnant of people who have not bowed their knees to Baal (See 1 Kings 19)! But I truly believe that when God begins to intercept these demonic technologies and behavior patterns among His leaders we shall see greater dimensions of revival in the Body of Christ. God wants to intercept the "snakes in our money bags" that are robbing us of our divine destiny, while bringing shame to the cause of Christ. I know that ministry takes money, especially effective life giving ministry. This is why I asked God to give me a "stronghold of resources" from the marketplace. I launched a company called "Kingdom Marketplace Coalition LLC," a social networking and educational portal which is growing by leaps and bounds because I told God that I did not want to undersell my apostolic calling to the "Almighty dollar!"

> *God wants to intercept the "snakes in our money bags" that are robbing us of our divine destiny, while bringing shame to the cause of Christ.*

Some might say, "Dr. Myles why are you involved in running a business when you are a pastor?" This question might have made sense if I was operating under a Levitical mindset and priestly order, but I live and operate under the Order of Melchizedek, which is a kingly-priestly order. Under this eternal order senior pastors can receive grace to be effective pastors while running a profitable business in the peripherals of the marketplace. There are too many five-fold ministers of the gospel who depend entirely on the "tithes and offerings" of workplace saints. This was once my portion until the Holy Spirit introduced me to the Order of Melchizedek (Gen. 14).

LIFE APPLICATION SECTION

MEMORY VERSE

So Abram left Egypt and traveled north into the Negev, along with his wife and Lot and all that they owned. [2] (Abram was very rich in livestock, silver, and gold.) Genesis 13:1-2

REFLECTIONS

What is your understanding of the phrase "Snakes in Money Bags?"

_____
_____
_____
_____
_____
_____

How did Abram's actions in Egypt affect his relationship with his nephew, Lot?

_____
_____
_____
_____
_____
_____

JOURNAL YOUR THOUGHTS

_____
_____
_____
_____
_____
_____
_____
_____
_____
_____
_____
_____
_____
_____
_____
_____
_____
_____
_____
_____
_____
_____
_____
_____
_____
_____
_____
_____
_____
_____
_____
_____

SNAKES IN MONEY BAGS

CHAPTER SIX
THE INTERCEPTION

In this chapter, I will go into the depths of the primary assignment of this writing. This book is my humble attempt to explain and introduce you to one of the greatest spiritual technologies in all of creation, the technology of divine interception. Even though this technology is ancient and many Kingdom citizens do not know how to cooperate with it, it is a very common concept in the world of sports. In the world of sports there is no word that is more powerful and generates more excitement or anxiety than the word INTERCEPTION. In the National Football League (NFL) offensive coaches spend countless hours priming their quarterbacks against throwing an interception. On the other hand, defensive coaches spend countless hours priming their defensive backs on how to intercept throws made by the opposing team's quarterback.

In January 2010, the Minnesota Vikings led by legendary quarterback and future Hall of Famer Brett Favre went into New Orleans, Louisiana to face-off with the New Orleans Saints for the right to go to the Super Bowl. In the last few seconds before the end of the game everything was going in favor of the Minnesota Vikings, who just needed to gain five more yards to clinch a spot in the Super Bowl. But as fate would have it, legendary quarterback Brett Favre's final throw was intercepted by one of the New Orleans Saints defensive backs. This interception dashed the Super Bowl hopes of the Vikings, but it resurrected the Super Bowl hopes of the Saints. Without the interception made by the New Orleans Saints defensive back the Super Bowl trophy that sits in the city of New Orleans today, would not have been possible.

In this chapter I will take this common concept of interception and expand it beyond its application to the world of sports. In the realms of the Spirit, interception technology is one of the most powerful and lethal spiritual technologies. In the next chapter I will show you in greater detail the difference between the technology of divine interception and the technology of divine intervention. There are those who would say that these spiritual technologies are one and the same. Nothing could be further from the truth, and not understanding their critical differences has led many Kingdom citizens into unnecessary spiritual battles with the enemy.

> *After Abram returned from his victory over Kedorlaomer and all his allies, the king of Sodom went out to meet him in the valley of Shaveh (that is, the King's Valley). And Melchizedek, the king of Salem and a priest of God Most High, brought Abram some bread and wine. Melchizedek blessed Abram with this blessing: "Blessed be Abram by God Most High, Creator of heaven and earth. And blessed be God Most High, who has defeated your enemies for you." Then Abram gave Melchizedek a tenth of all the goods he had recovered. Genesis 14:17-20*

Politically and socially we are living in very dangerous times. The sovereignty of nations is constantly being threatened by international terrorism. For many of us who live in the United States, we will never forget the horrors of September 11, 2001, which brought the portals of terror right to our doorsteps. Rogue nation dictators, such as in North Korea and Iran, are determined to build nuclear weapons, and are telling the world that they want to wipe Israel off the face of the earth.

> *In the realms of the Spirit, interception technology is one of the most powerful and lethal spiritual technologies.*

The growing threat of terrorism posed by the rapid rise of radical Islamists and the rise of rogue dictators has forced world powers like the United States of America, Great Britain, Russia, and China to invest heavily in nuclear missile interception technology. This technology specializes in enhancing the ability of nations to intercept nuclear missiles that might be launched against them by some fanatical terrorists. This technology has given nations such as the United States the military capability to defuse a nuclear missile in midair, rendering it useless in regard to its original objective.

> *Lot went into Sodom a wealthy righteous man, but he came out a financially bankrupt and backslidden preacher of righteousness.*

Thousands of years before the powers of the West thought of developing this powerful technology, God had already secured this spiritual technology for His Kingdom citizens.

According to Roget's Dictionary, *Intercept* means:

1. To take, seize, or halt (someone or something on the way from one place to another); cut off from an intended destination: to intercept a messenger.

2. To see or overhear (a message, transmission, etc., meant for another).

3. To stop or check (passage, travel, etc.) to intercept the traitor's escape.

4. To take possession of (a ball or puck) during an attempted pass by an opposing team.

5. To stop or interrupt the course, progress, or transmission of.

6. To destroy or disperse (enemy aircraft or a missile or missiles) in the air on the way to a target.

7. To stop the natural course of (light, water, etc.).

8. To intersect.

9. Obsolete. To prevent or cut off the operation or effect of.

10. Obsolete. To cut off from access, sight, etc.

I hope that you are as excited as I am about the far-reaching spiritual implications of what it means for you and I to be *intercepted* by God before we are overrun by a demonic nuclear missile. *Divine interception means that God apprehends us before we get taken by the enemy!* After Abram soundly defeated the kings from the East that had plundered Sodom, news of his resounding victory reached the ears of the king of Sodom. The king of Sodom quickly informed the keeper of his royal chariots to mount his horses because they were going to intercept Abram on his return. The king of Sodom put on his royal garments and fumed himself in the oils and fragrances which were offered in worship to his demon gods. With the smell of hell oozing from his body, the king of Sodom drove his chariots like a mad race-car driver to the finish line. He was in a demonic hurry to intercept Abram, but he was too late.

Moments before the king of Sodom and his diplomatic entourage from the land of Sodom arrived, Melchizedek, High Priest of God Most High, intercepted Abram. Many scholars believe that this King-Priest was a pre-incarnation manifestation of Christ. This priestly man, who was also the prophetic representation of the eternal priesthood of our Lord Jesus Christ, intercepted Abram just before the king of Sodom got to him. The divine encounter between Abram and Melchizedek was so powerful and life changing that Abram did something that he had never done before. *"Abram gave this Priest of God Most High, his first tithe..."* I have also discussed these tithes of honor in great detail in my book, *The Return of the Lost Key: Tithing under the Order of Melchizedek.* What is very important to understand is that Abram would have fallen to the seductive power of the king of Sodom had he not been intercepted by the priesthood of Melchizedek. This means that Abram's future destiny was only possible because of what God saved him from through this divine interception.

Do Not Make a Deal with the King of Sodom

Moments after Melchizedek's departure, the chariots of the king of Sodom screeched to a halt, shooting speckles of dust into the air. The king of Sodom dismounted and in royal pomp walked over to Abram. The king of Sodom had heard of Abram but he had never met him until now. The king of Sodom gave Abram a hideous smile and offered him a deal that he felt Abram could not refuse. Had the king of Sodom succeeded in manipulating Abram into signing the demonic contract, God would have had to look for another man to do what He had called Abram to do. This is how serious the confrontation between Abram and the king of Sodom was to Abram's future destiny and God's purpose for humankind.

The king of Sodom told Abram to give his people back. But he told Abram he could keep the money that the foreign invaders had stolen from the treasuries of Sodom. If Abram had been like some of today's ecclesiastical and marketplace ministers he would have taken the bounty from the treasuries of Sodom. He would have televised it as testimony of a great financial miracle. Fortunately Abram had just been introduced to the Order of Melchizedek. This one encounter with the Order of Melchizedek had opened his spiritual eyes and helped his spirit to properly discern the king of Sodom's hidden demonic agenda. In a prophetic sense, Abram saw all the poisonous snakes that were hidden in the money bags that the king of Sodom was offering him. Had Abram taken the money from the treasuries of Sodom, he would have opened a spiritual portal for devils to enter his life.

> *Moments before the king of Sodom and his diplomatic entourage from the land of Sodom arrived, Melchizedek, High Priest of God Most High, intercepted Abram.*

How many great spiritual leaders and Kingdom businessmen do you know who have caved in to the king of Sodom? Some spiritual leaders and businessmen are selling their souls to demonic systems for an extra buck! The scandalous fall of great televangelists in the 1980s and 1990s rocked the entire church world. The men who were heading these ministries failed to say "NO" to the seductive offers of the king of Sodom. In light of such scandals that have tarnished the image of the Church and hurt the cause of Christ, you cannot convince me that spiritual leaders in the Body of Christ do not need to submit themselves to the Order of Melchizedek.

Instead of taking the money the king of Sodom had offered him, Abram emphatically and publicly told the king of Sodom that his answer was a resounding and heartfelt, "NO!" Abram told the king of Sodom that there was nothing he owned in all of Sodom that Abram desired for himself or his ministry. *This means that there is a "more excellent way" of acquiring "real Kingdom wealth" without compromising Kingdom values and principles.* Abram then proceeded to tell the king of Sodom the two main reasons why he had turned down his demonically engineered offer.

The first reason revealed the source of Abram's power.

Abram replied to the king of Sodom, "I solemnly swear to the Lord, God Most High, Creator of heaven and earth, that I will not take so much as a single thread or sandal thong from what belongs to you... Genesis 14:22-23

The main reason Abram refused the offer of money from the hands of the king of Sodom was based upon the fact that he had just *established a covenant of tithe* with God through Melchizedek who was the Priest of God Most High. This one divine encounter with Melchizedek's priesthood had shown him that God was his source for everything he needed to fulfill the prophetic assignment upon his life. *This awesome encounter with the heavenly King-Priest had completely shut down the wells of greed inside the chambers of his sanctified soul.* The glitter of the gold and silver from the treasuries of Sodom had suddenly lost their lustrous appeal. Abram was a changed man.

The second reason unmasked the hidden demonic agenda behind the offer of the king of Sodom.

...Otherwise you might say, 'I am the one who made Abram rich.'
Genesis 14:23

The second reason that underscores why Abram refused to take money from the hands of the king of Sodom was based upon another very important consideration. Abram knew through personal experience that when you take money from the devil there will always be hell to pay in the near future! Abram had made a similar mistake when he stretched out his hands to take the gold and silver that the king of Egypt had offered him.

Years later after Abram took the "hush money" from the treasuries of the king of Egypt, he was stalked constantly by rumors which said that the king of Egypt was boasting and telling people that he was the one who had made Abram rich. These stories caused Abram tremendous pain and embarrassment. Fortunately when the king of Sodom showed up and offered him the same deal, he was able to discern that this particular financial offer by the king of Sodom was more sinister and spiritually poisonous than that of the king of Egypt. The covenant communion of the sacred bread and wine that he had received at the hands of Melchizedek had infused him with a keen sense of spiritual awareness and discernment! This is why New Testament believers need to be aware of what is available to them under the eternal priestly Order that our Lord Jesus Christ presides over.

SNAKES IN MONEY BAGS

Abram's ability to reject the generous offer that was offered by the king of Sodom also has far-reaching spiritual ramifications for the seed of Abram. According to the principle of apostolic succession, we were all (born-again believers) in the spiritual loins of Abram when he said "NO" to the king of Sodom and rose above the seductive power of the gold and silver of this world. This means that if we tap into the same grace that Abram discovered when he met Melchizedek, the seductive power of mammon will be broken over our lives and business practices! Nevertheless, this will not happen unless we become accurately connected to the Order of Melchizedek.

> *Abram knew through personal experience that when you take money from the devil there will always be hell to pay in the near future!*

Nothing has destroyed more good ministries and businessmen than the seductive and corrupting influence of money and sex. The corridors of human history are plastered with tragic stories of great men and women of God who had great world-shaking ministries. But some of these servants of God and their ministries were destroyed when they failed to say, "NO" to the king of Sodom. During the apex of their success story and national notoriety, the chariots of the king of Sodom (the devil) stopped at their doorsteps. *The king of Sodom made them an offer they failed to refuse.* The scandalous fall of their ministries now plagues us all.

Some great ministries that are commanding a large following presently have also fallen to the power of the king of Sodom. They have become contaminated by the demonic sodomic system. Even though examining their mega ministry from the outside may look very appealing to the undiscerning eye, the process of spiritual decline in the lives of these modern-day gospel greats has already begun. *Only God and the devil know that they are carrying snakes in their money bags.* The machinery of death is already at work in the internal matrix of their ministries or businesses, and they are more glamorous than glorious.

Nothing can open demonic portals for devils to enter our life like inaccurate patterns of unlocking financial resources for our ministry or business. We must remember that just because something works does not mean it is right. We can manipulate the saints or business partners for money and make them give us whatever we want. This demonic behavior in us will only set us up for death and destruction in our future destiny.

> *Nothing can open demonic portals for devils to enter our life and ministry like inaccurate patterns of unlocking financial resources for our ministry or business.*

Please remember that Abram and Lot became very wealthy almost overnight when Abram lied to Pharaoh. Abram told the king of Egypt that Sarai was his sister instead of his wife. The king of Egypt, with a mouth dripping with sexual lust for Sarai, gave Abram and Lot an abundance of gold, silver, livestock, and male and female servants. *For a short season, Abram's lie worked miracles for him.* He got blessed by cheating a king and manipulating his wife into lying against her own conscience.

Abram left Egypt with the bounty he had made by lying to Pharaoh and placing his wife in a very compromising situation. Abram thought he got away with it. Nothing could have been further from the truth. Resources gained from using demonic technology always come filled with snakes. These demonically engineered snakes are preprogrammed by the enemy to strike and inject us with their poison at a strategic time in our future destiny when we are most vulnerable. This attack of the enemy usually happens at a time when the devil knows that he can cause the most damage to the cause of Christ.

One of the snakes that was in one of the money bags that the king of Egypt gave to Abram was a young Egyptian maid named Hagar. *The devil had set her up as his trump card. She was a ticking time bomb in Abram's future destiny.* When she finally exploded in Abram and Sarai's lives, she produced an Ishmael in Abram's bloodline. The consequences of this costly mistake in Abram's life are still being felt and played out on the global scene thousands of years later as evidenced each day in the news media. Reports of continuing violent clashes between Palestinian Arabs (the natural descendants of Abram's Ishmael) and neighboring Jews in Israel are commonplace.

THE INTERCEPTION

In the case of Abram's Ishmael, God intervened to move him away from Isaac, the child of promise. God used Sarai to initiate the process of moving Ishmael from the place of proximity with Isaac. Sarai saw Ishmael mocking her son Isaac, and it grieved her deeply. She went to Abram and demanded that he send Hagar and her son into exile. Abram was very grieved when he heard the news because he loved Ishmael very much, but God showed up and supported Sarai's decision. This story illustrates the critical difference between divine interception and divine intervention. I will explain in greater detail this critical difference between the two spiritual technologies in the next chapter.

LIFE APPLICATION SECTION

MEMORY VERSE

After Abram returned from his victory over Kedorlaomer and all his allies, the king of Sodom went out to meet him in the valley of Shaveh (that is, the King's Valley). And Melchizedek, the king of Salem and a priest of God Most High, brought Abram some bread and wine. Melchizedek blessed Abram with this blessing: "Blessed be Abram by God Most High, Creator of heaven and earth. And blessed be God Most High, who has defeated your enemies for you." Then Abram gave Melchizedek a tenth of all the goods he had recovered. Genesis 14:17-20

REFLECTIONS

Who intercepted Abram in the Valley of the Kings?

_____

_____

_____

_____

_____

_____

Why did this eternal King-Priest intercept Abram?

_____

_____

_____

_____

_____

_____

THE INTERCEPTION

JOURNAL YOUR THOUGHTS

CHAPTER SEVEN
INTERCEPTION VERSUS
INTERVENTION

This chapter is probably one of the most important chapters in this whole book - so much that I felt this chapter deserved the combined insights of two apostolic voices. So I asked my dear friend Dr. Gordon Bradshaw, apostolic founder of Voice of God Ministries in Dolton, Illinois to co-author this intrinsic chapter with me. This chapter was born out of our combined apostolic contemplation and prayer. We asked God to help us handle the subject of this chapter with the prayerful and surgical sensitivity that it truly deserves.

There is an old saying... *"An ounce of prevention is worth a pound of cure."* Nothing demonstrates this concept better than the example that the Fire Department uses to stress the importance of fire safety and the preventive measures that go with it. It is good to have a well prepared and trained fire department in a community. A great deal of time and money are spent preparing the firefighters to respond quickly to the report of a fire. On arrival, the firefighters put their years of expertise to work to save lives and property. The people who do this type of work are often hailed as heroes, and they very much are. But is the work of the firefighter at the scene of a fire the best solution to produce a safe community, or is there a better way? There is a group of firefighters known as the fire prevention bureau. People don't speak of them often and they aren't seen speeding to an emergency to save lives and property. It's a rather quiet job, but it is more important than many realize. This team provides public education, training for school children, public safety demonstrations, pamphlets and inspections of property to ensure that the public is trained on how to *prevent* fires from starting. Their work is the technology of *"interception"* rather than the technology of *"intervention."* Firefighters who actually respond to fires provide *"intervention"* and are always faced with a dangerous situation that is already in progress.

When a fire is reported, the firefighters respond, but the problem is… there is already a fire that is currently damaging property and threatening lives, even the lives of the firefighters themselves. Even if the firefighters are fast and efficient, there is bound to be irreversible damage of some kind due to the fire that is already in progress. A good fire prevention and inspection program turns around many disasters and saves millions of dollars in property damage by *"intercepting"* the cause of fires before they occur. When people are aware of how to properly prevent fires, they become part of the fire prevention team and everyone benefits.

INTERVENTION AS AN INTENTIONAL TECHNOLOGY

Intervention becomes an *"Intentional"* technology of God when He allows situations to occur to benefit His ultimate will and purpose. One such example is found in John 11:1-45 and it contains the story of Lazarus. Jesus was informed of Lazarus' sickness in verses *3-4*. *"Therefore his sisters sent unto him, saying, Lord, behold, he whom thou lovest is sick. When Jesus heard that, he said, This sickness is not unto death, but for the glory of God, that the Son of God might be glorified thereby."*

Verses *17-21* point out that Lazarus was already dead. Martha, the sister of Lazarus made a statement that further indicates that this case was about to become a powerful demonstration of God's chosen technology of *"intervention."*

"Then when Jesus came, he found that he had lain in the grave four days already. Now Bethany was night unto Jerusalem, about fifteen furlongs off: And many of the Jews came to Martha and Mary, to comfort them concerning their brother. Then Martha, as soon as she heard that Jesus was coming, went out and met him: but Mary sat still in the house. Then said Martha unto Jesus, Lord, if thou hadst been here, my brother had not died."

Lazarus' sister Martha was hoping that Jesus would exercise *"Divine Interception"* in this case. However, he chose a different route. Verses 39-44 finish the account by revealing the full purpose of God's decision to use *"intervention"* instead of *"interception"* in this case.

"Jesus said, Take away the stone. Martha, the sister of him that was dead, saith unto him, Lord, by this time he stinketh: for he hath been dead four days. Jesus saith unto her, 'Said I not unto thee, that, if thou wouldest believe, that thou shouldest see the glory of God?' Then they took away the stone from the place where the dead was laid. And Jesus lifted up his eyes and said, 'Father, I thank thee that thou hast heard me. And I knew that thou hearest me always: but because of the people which stand by I said it, that they may believe that thou hast sent me.' And when he had thus spoken, he cried with a loud voice, 'Lazarus, come forth.' And he that was dead came forth, bound hand and foot with graveclothes: and his face was bound about with a napkin. Jesus saith unto them, 'Loose him; and let him go.'"

It is obvious that Jesus has the power of life in His words. Therefore the fact that Lazarus died before Jesus could get to him was irrelevant. Jesus was able to allow death to reach Lazarus and still exercise total dominion over how long death could hold him. He did this entirely to produce the case that has served as one of the most powerful resurrection scenarios of all time! Most importantly, Lazarus's story presents us with one of the best biblical case studies of the critical difference between the "technology of divine interception and the technology of divine intervention." But we will look at more biblical case studies about the operational differences between these two spiritual technologies.

INTERCEPTION VERSUS INTERVENTION

DEFINING THE TWO TECHNOLOGIES

The thesaurus dictionary defines "Interception" as *"the engaging of an enemy force in an attempt to hinder or prevent it from carrying out its mission."* But it defines "Intervention" as follows: *"to interfere, usually through force or threat of force, in the affairs of another nation."* It is clear that even the dictionary acknowledges that there is a critical difference between these two words, but when they are examined as "spiritual technologies" the differences between them are staggering.

When interception and intervention are compared side-by-side as spiritual technologies, they are supremely different. It is thus extremely important for us to understand this critical distinction and difference, for otherwise we may open ourselves to great loss and heartache if we confuse, misunderstand or misapply what God has already separated. So I (Dr. Myles) will give you the spiritual definitions of these two technologies that the Lord gave me.

The Holy Spirit said "DIVINE INTERCEPTION"…

- Is the preemptive technology of the Kingdom of God

- Means that God will take us "IN" before the enemy has had a chance to take "US OUT"

- Is the technology of providing the answer before the question is ever asked

- Is the technology of providing the solution before the problem

- Is the most powerful spiritual technology in all of creation

- Is the only technology of warfare that guarantees victory without bloodshed or loss on the part of the person who is being intercepted

- Is a higher spiritual technology than the technology of divine intervention

- Is based upon God's foreknowledge, which is why interception technology is one of the most powerful spiritual technologies in all of creation

The Holy Spirit said "DIVINE INTERVENTION"...

- Is the technology of rescue that services Kingdom citizens in the field of battle

- Means that God will take "US OUT" after the enemy has taken us "IN"

- Is the technology of combative warfare

- Is the spiritual technology for providing the answer after the question has already been asked

- Does not guarantee the absence of bloodshed or loss in the life of the person or business that is in need of divine intervention

- Is usually initiated by God after His people fail to respond in total obedience to the technology of divine interception

- Is based upon the sovereign power of God

"DIVINE INTERCEPTION"... Is the preemptive technology of the Kingdom of God.

It is quite clear from the above definitions that the technology of divine interception and the technology of divine intervention are two completely different spiritual technologies. Even though these technologies are both divinely inspired, they are as different as male and female. God told me that if my people do not know how to distinguish between these two spiritual technologies they will live in an endless cycle of drama. There will always be moments of divine intervention, but God does not want His people to become addicted to *"divine intervention."* A life built around divine interception is a more excellent way of living than a life built around divine intervention.

God showed me that His people have become like "Deliverance junkies" in their addiction to the technology of divine intervention. His people have become so used to drama or living from crisis to crisis that they have become addicted to divine intervention. Many believers feel like divine intervention is a sign of their spirituality or favor with God. But nothing could be further from the truth, because more often than not, divine intervention only becomes necessary because there has been no prior obedience to the technology of divine interception. I really believe that our spiritual maturity in the Kingdom is directly connected to our ability to yield accurately and consistently to the technology of divine interception. It takes more spiritual maturity to obey God before we are in a crisis than it takes to obey God when we are in trouble and our house is on fire.

> *"DIVINE INTERVENTION"... Is the technology of rescue that services Kingdom citizens in the field of battle.*

We will now examine some biblical case studies that will show us the difference between the technology of divine interception and the technology of divine intervention. These biblical stories will enforce the critical importance of the technology of divine interception in the lives of Kingdom citizens.

DREAMS OF A PARADISE LOST

Then the LORD God planted a garden in Eden in the east, and there he placed the man he had made. ⁹ The LORD God made all sorts of trees grow up from the ground—trees that were beautiful and that produced delicious fruit. In the middle of the garden he placed the tree of life and the tree of the knowledge of good and evil. Genesis 2:8-9

The LORD God placed the man in the Garden of Eden to tend and watch over it. [16] But the LORD God warned him, "You may freely eat the fruit of every tree in the garden—[17] except the tree of the knowledge of good and evil. If you eat its fruit, you are sure to die." Genesis 2:15-17

The book of Genesis describes the origins of the species called humankind and also exposes the divine intent for the creation of a physical planet. Contrary to the teaching of modern science, the presence of humankind on planet Earth has nothing to with Darwin's hypothesis of evolution. Darwin's hypothesis is unscientific and has now been largely discredited by many credible scientists. Ben Stiller, in his famed movie *Evolution: No Intelligence Allowed*, exposes the glaring flaws behind Darwin's hypothesis of evolution and reveals the diabolical conspiracy to silence and discredit scientists and educators who strongly disagree with Darwin's outdated and unscientific hypothesis by liberal scholars with a Godless agenda.

The Genesis account tells us that Adam and Eve, the first Kingdom ambassadors, were given a governor's mansion in the center of a garden of tremendous abundance. While they were living in this garden of abundance they lacked for nothing. The only condition of residency that God placed on them to retain this position of power and prominence was to resist the temptation to eat from the tree of the knowledge of good and evil.

God was very explicit in his instruction. He told them that the day they ate of the forbidden tree they would die. *Whichever way you squeeze this, it would seem to me that God was introducing the first couple to the technology of divine interception.* It seems to me that God was trying to save them from experiencing the pain and loss that is associated with the technology of Death. But instead of yielding to the technology of divine interception, the first ambassadorial couple chose to listen to an unemployed cherubim (Lucifer) living in exile and the rest is history. A panoramic view of the devastation that sin and death have brought to bear on our troubled planet is undeniable evidence of the importance of yielding in total obedience to the technology of divine interception, whenever and wherever God initiates it.

So the Lord God banished them from the Garden of Eden, and he sent Adam out to cultivate the ground from which he had been made. After sending them out, the Lord God stationed mighty cherubim to the east of the Garden of Eden. And he placed a flaming sword that flashed back and forth to guard the way to the tree of life. Genesis 3:23-24

The fall of Adam and Eve, the first regent kings on behalf of God's government over the colony called Earth, forced God to evict them from the governor's mansion in the Garden of Eden. God could no longer trust them with the stewardship of Eden's paradise. They were driven out of this supernatural garden of abundance and were subjected to a life of endless toil and sweat outside God's paradise (Kingdom). Even though God's mercy atoned for their transgression when God killed an innocent animal and covered them in its blood, they realized that the cost of responding to divine interception is much less than the cost of going through divine intervention.

Lucifer, an unemployed cherub who had been cast out of heaven, became the de facto king of this world! I believe it was during this time when the kingdoms (systems) of finance, business, law, celebration/sports, media, family, and church fell into the hands of demonic powers. This explains why God warned the first couple that if they lost their ambassadorial position over the earthly colony they would have to "toil and sweat" for all their daily needs. Since the fall of the first ambassadorial couple, the devil will not allow God's people easy access to the mountains of finance, business, media, law, celebration/sports, family, and church, without intense warfare. I think you would agree with me that had Adam and Eve responded to divine interception, life on earth would have been very different. All of the suffering and poverty that we see around the world would have been completely avoided.

ABRAM'S MEETING WITH MELCHIZEDEK

And Melchizedek, the king of Salem and a priest of God Most High, brought Abram some bread and wine. [19] Melchizedek blessed Abram with this blessing: "Blessed be Abram by God

Most High, Creator of heaven and earth.[20] And blessed be God Most High, who has defeated your enemies for you." Then Abram gave Melchizedek a tenth of all the goods he had recovered. [21] The king of Sodom said to Abram, "Give back my people who were captured. But you may keep for yourself all the goods you have recovered." [22] Abram replied to the king of Sodom, "I solemnly swear to the LORD, God Most High, Creator of heaven and earth, [23] that I will not take so much as a single thread or sandal thong from what belongs to you. Otherwise you might say, 'I am the one who made Abram rich.' Genesis 14:18-23

When Abram was returning from the slaughter of the foreign kings, he was intercepted by a man who was to alter the course of Abram's life. When Abram met this majestic man, he began to realize by inspiration and revelation that meeting this heavenly-man was what every road in his life had been leading up to. Abram had by divine orchestration entered into the moment of moments. The mystery of God was about to be revealed. *Time and eternity were about to embrace. The promise-bearer was about to meet the promise-giver. The day of interception had finally arrived.*

> **The cost of responding to divine interception is much less than the cost of going through divine intervention.**

There was a divine aura and deep sense of dignity upon this man that Abram had never seen or felt before. From his feet to the hair on his head this heavenly-man exhibited a sense of divinity and righteousness that was overpowering. Abram realized that this man was the greatest and most important man he would ever meet here on earth. I believe that Abram could sense that this man was the same God who had provided information which delivered his wife from the bedchamber of the king of Egypt. Abram knew this interception would leave an indelible mark on his life forever.

DEMONICALLY ENGINEERED INTERCEPTIONS

After Abram returned from his victory over Kedorlaomer and all his allies, the king of Sodom went out to meet him in the valley of Shaveh (that is, the King's Valley). Genesis 14:17

While Abram was returning from the slaughter of the kings from the East, news of his glorious victory also reached the ears of the king of Sodom. The king of Sodom drove in his royal chariot to intercept Abram on his victorious return. *The "king of Sodom" represents a demonic system that wants to entrap Kingdom businessmen and women in the marketplace.* Abram did not know that the king of Sodom was riding ferociously toward him, but the Lord did. The setting and timing God chose to introduce Abram to the priestly Order of Melchizedek is very significant indeed. The perfect spiritual timing of Melchizedek's appearance in Abram's life will shed light on the awesome power of this eternal priestly order. The Order of Melchizedek is saturated with the technology of divine interception. It was no coincidence that God in His infinite wisdom chose to intercept Abram's life just before the king of Sodom reached him. *God was determined to reach Abram before the devil's greatest agent did. God was determined to take Abram in before the devil took him out.*

The devil has enough sense to know that whatever God does is always successful. The devil knows that God is the root and origin of every successful principle and life-giving technology in all of creation. This is why the devil is a master at counterfeiting the principles and technologies of the Kingdom of God. Since the devil knows that interception technology is a very powerful technology of conquest, he has also established demonically engineered interceptions. This would explain why the devil usually shows up as an angel of light in people's lives just before God sends them their true spiritual inheritance.

> *The "king of Sodom" represents a demonic system that wants to entrap Kingdom businessmen and women in the marketplace.*

The phenomenon of demonically engineered interceptions is one of the numerous reasons why many Kingdom citizens end up marrying the wrong person. In most cases, the rush to get married causes many believers to challenge the technology of divine interception that was telling them to wait for their God ordained partner before saying I do. I have met so many highly anointed men and women of God in the ministry who are married to spouses who have no desire for ministry and never did from the get-go. I asked God why this phenomenon in the ministry is so common and God showed me that this is the fruit of disobedience to the technology of divine interception. If the truth were told, many of these anointed men and women of God married out of sexual appeal without considering the long term effects of such a decision on their God-given destiny. This is why the divorce rate in the church is as high as the world's because many Kingdom citizens are choosing their life partners on the basis of sexual appeal, instead of allowing the Holy Spirit to match them with a person who is divinely fashioned by God for their destiny.

Having said what I believe needed to be said, in order to intercept single brothers and sisters from choosing the wrong mate, I want to state emphatically that if you are already married, do not use my writing as a license to divorce your spouse because you feel like you made a wrong choice. Our God is a covenant keeping God and He honors the covenant of marriage that you are in right now. So whether you feel like you made the right or wrong choice is irrelevant at this point. What is important is that God through the technology of divine intervention can take a marriage full of sour grapes and transform it into a vineyard of endless blessings.

The demonic phenomenon of persons of destiny being married to spouses who have no passion for destiny, parallels many of the demonic business partnerships that many Kingdom entrepreneurs find themselves involved with in the marketplace. Many demonically engineered interceptions that lure many Kingdom businessmen and women into demonic business partnerships that translate into bad business deals are getting ready to be intercepted by God. The Kingdom of God will not continue to lose millions of dollars in Kingdom resources to demonic powers because of the lack of divine interception in the lives of many

Kingdom entrepreneurs. If you have a marketplace ministry (you are either a Joseph or Daniel, Esther or Lydia), God is about to saturate your vehicle of commerce with the technology of divine interception.

LOT'S RESCUE

As it happened, the valley of the Dead Sea was filled with tar pits. And as the army of the kings of Sodom and Gomorrah fled, some fell into the tar pits, while the rest escaped into the mountains. [11] The victorious invaders then plundered Sodom and Gomorrah and headed for home, taking with them all the spoils of war and the food supplies. [12] They also captured Lot—Abram's nephew who lived in Sodom—and carried off everything he owned. Genesis 13:10-12

Long after Lot's migration to the wicked nation of Sodom, five powerful kings from the East came against the king of Sodom and ravaged his country. In their victory these foreign kings took men, women, and children as prisoners of war. They also emptied the treasuries of Sodom of most of its gold and silver. Lot, Abram's nephew, was among the prisoners of war who were taken captive by the invading horde. A man who had escaped the rampage ran to the house of Abram the Hebrew and told him that Lot had been captured by the armies of the kings from the East.

When Abram heard that his nephew Lot had been captured, he mobilized the 318 trained men who had been born into his household. Then he pursued Kedorlaomer's army until he caught up with them at Dan. [15] There he divided his men and attacked during the night. Kedorlaomer's army fled, but Abram chased them as far as Hobah, north of Damascus. [16] Abram recovered all the goods that had been taken, and he brought back his nephew Lot with his possessions and all the women and other captives. Genesis 13:14-16

Abram rose in haste and dressed himself for war. He assembled an army of about 318 men who were born and trained in his own house.

He was also joined by a few of his allies. With the determination of an Olympic sprinter, Abram pursued the kings who had captured his nephew and family. In less than twenty-four hours, Abram and his men overtook the foreign armies. Abram slaughtered these formidable enemy combatants with his homegrown force of men! Abram rescued all of his family members, including all the people of Sodom who had been taken captive. Abram also brought back all the gold and silver that these foreign kings had taken from the treasuries of Sodom.

The story of Lot's rescue by Abram from the hands of the Babylonian kings who had attacked Sodom where Lot and his family were living, showcases the critical difference between the technology of divine interception and the technology of divine intervention. Divine intervention is almost always a rescue mission. All rescue missions operate on the premise that a "Crisis" is already in progress and needs to be contained before the damage becomes irreparable.

I'm very sure that by the time Abram rescued Lot and his family from captivity, Lot and his family had already gone through much pain and suffering. Lot had to endure the pain and shame of seeing his family mistreated by the foreign invaders, while he looked on helplessly. Imagine the shame that must have blanketed this righteous man when he was dragged away like cattle by the invading hordes from the East. It was very embarrassing to say the least. But God's mercy initiated the technology of divine intervention to rescue Lot and his family from the hands of these foreign invaders.

Divine intervention is almost always a rescue mission.

I want to set the record straight; even though I am making the argument that the technology of divine interception is a higher technology of the Kingdom of God than the technology of divine intervention, I am not diminishing the importance of the technology of divine intervention. Many of us are currently caught up in a whirlwind of pain and suffering induced by our own bad choices from our immediate past. If God in His mercy did not initiate the technology of divine intervention, the spiritual ramifications of our disobedience and bad choices would completely annihilate our God-given destiny on the planet. This is why for those of us who are already in a storm of trouble, the technology of divine intervention is more important at this point than the technology of divine interception. My purpose in writing this book is to minimize or eliminate unnecessary moments of divine intervention. Life is too short to be wasted in a saga of unending and unfruitful drama.

PHARAOH'S DREAMS

Two full years later, Pharaoh dreamed that he was standing on the bank of the Nile River. [2] In his dream he saw seven fat, healthy cows come up out of the river and begin grazing in the marsh grass. [3] Then he saw seven more cows come up behind them from the Nile, but these were scrawny and thin. These cows stood beside the fat cows on the riverbank. [4] Then the scrawny, thin cows ate the seven healthy, fat cows! At this point in the dream, Pharaoh woke up. [5] But he fell asleep again and had a second dream. This time he saw seven heads of grain, plump and beautiful, growing on a single stalk. [6] Then seven more heads of grain appeared, but these were shriveled and withered by the east wind. [7] And these thin heads swallowed up the seven plump, well-formed heads! Then Pharaoh woke up again and realized it was a dream. [8] The next morning Pharaoh was very disturbed by the dreams. So he called for all the magicians and wise men of Egypt. When Pharaoh told them his dreams, not one of them could tell him what they meant. Genesis 41:1-8

The prophetic dreams that God gave to Pharaoh during Joseph's era in Egypt are probably some of the most well-known prophetic dreams. Epic movies about the life of Joseph have been produced by Hollywood,with special sound and visual effects. Many might say that the reason Pharaoh's prophetic dreams are so well known is because God used them to bring Joseph to the forefront of political power. I beg to disagree. I really believe that the reason Pharaoh's prophetic dreams are so well known is because God used them to demonstrate the incredible power of the technology of divine interception.

God was using Pharaoh's prophetic dreams to show us how much the technology of divine interception can guide the future and economy of an entire nation. Pharaoh's prophetic dreams were powerful because they were a vehicle of the most powerful spiritual technology in all of creation – a spiritual technology which can intercept the past, present and future in one stroke. The reason the magicians of Egypt could not interpret Pharaoh's prophetic dream was because it contained a spiritual technology that belonged to a Kingdom they did not belong to. This technology required a citizen of the Kingdom of God to decipher and download it into the economy of Egypt.

When Pharaoh finished recounting his prophetic dream to Joseph, Joseph knew by revelation that God wanted to intercept a future global calamity. God was providing the answer to the question before the question was asked. God was insulating the Egyptian economy from total collapse against a global economic recession before it even took place. How many world leaders would love to have access to a technology that can intercept the economic future of their country before there are signs of any recession within the markets? I believe that many sensible world leaders would pay vast sums of money to secure such a technology to protect their nation's engines of commerce.

When the seven years of famine came upon the nations the Egyptian economy, which had been intercepted by God, was the only economy that survived this very trying time. The Egyptian economy was experiencing prosperity at a time when the economies of every other nation under heaven were disintegrating. The only difference between the Egyptian economy and the economies of the other nations was rooted in Pharaoh's ability to yield to the technology of divine interception. Pharaoh could have ignored Joseph's interpretation of his dream, but he did not. He could have treated Joseph as a common slave and prisoner who could not give advice to the most powerful man in Egypt, but he did not. Instead he responded to the "technology of divine interception" in total obedience and God honored his obedience. When the seven years of famine came upon the nations, every nation on the planet other than Egypt was in dire need of divine intervention.

> *God was using Pharaoh's prophetic dreams to show us how much the technology of divine interception can guide the future and economy of an entire nation.*

JOSEPH'S THOUGHTS ON INTERCEPTION

"I am Joseph!" he said to his brothers. "Is my father still alive?" But his brothers were speechless! They were stunned to realize that Joseph was standing there in front of them. ⁴ "Please, come closer," he said to them. So they came closer. And he said again, "I am Joseph, your brother, whom you sold into slavery in Egypt. ⁵ But don't be upset, and don't be angry with yourselves for selling me to this place. It was God who sent me here ahead of you to preserve your lives. ⁶ This famine that has ravaged the land for two years will last five more years, and there will be neither plowing nor harvesting. ⁷ God has sent me ahead of you to keep you and your families alive and to preserve many survivors. Genesis 45:3-7

It is clear that Joseph was no stranger to the technology of divine interception. He was very much aware of the potency of this powerful spiritual technology. When his brothers in pursuit of divine intervention came to Egypt to buy wheat to sustain themselves and their livestock in the land of Canaan, Joseph began to appreciate the full ramifications of his presence in Egypt. He began to realize that the prophetic dreams he had as a young boy in the land of Canaan were vehicles of the technology of divine interception.

His dreams were no ordinary dreams. They were dreams that were designed to transport the technology of divine interception from the realms of eternity into the portals of time. God was actually intercepting the future in the now. Even though Joseph was heavily persecuted by his own brothers for being the host of such powerful dreams, he never let go of them. He held on to these prophetic dreams because he felt like they held keys to his future destiny. Thank God Joseph held on to these powerful prophetic dreams, because had he given up the whole world would have been extinguished by the ravaging famine. The human race was set for extinction had the devil succeeded in his diabolical agenda. But through Joseph God was able to intercept the full impact of what was a devastating global recession. When Joseph finally revealed himself to his brothers, he told them that "they meant to destroy him," but God used their jealousy to send him ahead of them to preserve a posterity for them.

INTERCEPTION TECHNOLOGY IN PAUL'S LIFE

Meanwhile, Saul was uttering threats with every breath and was eager to kill the Lord's followers. So he went to the high priest. [2] He requested letters addressed to the synagogues in Damascus, asking for their cooperation in the arrest of any followers of the Way he found there. He wanted to bring them—both men and women—back to Jerusalem in chains. [3] As he was approaching Damascus on this mission, a light from heaven suddenly shone down around him. [4] He fell to the ground and heard a voice saying to him, "Saul! Saul! Why are you persecuting me?" Acts 9:1-3

God knows that Paul the Apostle is my favorite writer of all time. I love to read the epistles of Paul. His life and revelation about the person of Christ never cease to fascinate me. Paul the Apostle was no stranger to the technology of divine interception, as well as intervention. Actually, Paul's dramatic conversion to Christ was the result of a God ordained moment of divine interception.

Paul was on his way to Damascus to persecute and arrest followers of Christ. He had obtained letters of authorization from the high priest to arrest followers of Christ in Damascus. Paul had already participated in the stoning of Stephen before moving on to Damascus. On his way to Damascus he was supernaturally intercepted by Christ himself. A shining light from heaven struck him and he fell from his horse. While he was on the ground he heard the voice of the resurrected Christ for the very first time. His life was completely turned around by this one encounter with the technology of divine interception. The interception was so dramatic that Paul never forgot it. It became the hallmark and reference point for the legitimacy of his apostolic ministry.

> **Paul the Apostle was no stranger to the technology of divine interception, as well as intervention.**

Several days later a man named Agabus, who also had the gift of prophecy, arrived from Judea. [11] He came over, took Paul's belt, and bound his own feet and hands with it. Then he said, "The Holy Spirit declares, 'So shall the owner of this belt be bound by the Jewish leaders in Jerusalem and turned over to the Gentiles.'" [12] When we heard this, we and the local believers all begged Paul not to go on to Jerusalem. [13] But he said, "Why all this weeping? You are breaking my heart! I am ready not only to be jailed at Jerusalem but even to die for the sake of the Lord Jesus." [14] When it was clear that we couldn't persuade him, we gave up and said, "The Lord's will be done." Acts 21:10-14

Even though the apostle Paul was no stranger to the power of the technology of divine interception, he did not yield to this technology in total obedience all the time. There were times when the great apostle to the church needed divine intervention, because he had failed to respond to divine interception. The most classic example of this is found in Acts 21:10-14. We will examine this passage of Scripture with forensic aptitude, so we can milk this story of the precious nuggets of truth that are contained in it.

The Bible tells us that there was a reputable prophet by the name of Agabus who was based in Judea. This powerful prophet of God came to visit the apostle Paul at Antioch. The prophet Agabus took Paul's belt and bound his own feet and hands with it. Then he began to prophesy by the Spirit what was going to happen to the apostle Paul if he went to Jerusalem. He prophesied that the owner of the belt that he held in his hands would be bound by Jewish religious leaders in Jerusalem and then thrown back to the Gentiles.

When Paul's apostolic ministerial staff heard the prophecy of this renowned prophet they begged Paul to heed the technology of divine interception. But the apostle Paul was so homesick he refused to heed the technology of divine interception that God was initiating on his behalf through the prophet Agabus. What is interesting is that Paul the Apostle managed to successfully spiritualize his disobedience to the technology of divine interception. He told his disciples who were begging him not to go to Jerusalem that he was more than ready to die for the Lord Jesus Christ. This would have been quite commendable had it been God's will for his life. But it was not God's will for Paul to go to Jerusalem or die in the city thereof. After Paul silenced the pleas of his ministerial staff he then embarked on a journey to Jerusalem.

Everything looked and seemed okay until Paul got to Jerusalem. Everything that could go wrong for Paul went wrong. We must remember that no matter our status in the economy of the Kingdom, if we refuse to respond to the technology of divine interception we will soon find ourselves in a situation which will demand that God deliver us through divine intervention.

INTERVENTION TECHNOLOGY IN PAUL'S LIFE

The next day Paul went with us to meet with James, and all the elders of the Jerusalem church were present. [19] After greeting them, Paul gave a detailed account of the things God had accomplished among the Gentiles through his ministry. [20] After hearing this, they praised God. And then they said, "You know, dear brother, how many thousands of Jews have also believed, and they all follow the law of Moses very seriously. [21] But the Jewish believers here in Jerusalem have been told that you are teaching all the Jews who live among the Gentiles to turn their backs on the laws of Moses. They've heard that you teach them not to circumcise their children or follow other Jewish customs. [22] What should we do? They will certainly hear that you have come.

[23] *"Here's what we want you to do. We have four men here who have completed their vow.* [24] *Go with them to the Temple and join them in the purification ceremony, paying for them to have their heads ritually shaved. Then everyone will know that the rumors are all false and that you yourself observe the Jewish laws. Acts 21:18-24*

When Paul arrived in Jerusalem he was welcomed warmly by the apostle James and all the elders of the church. After the customary greetings were over, Paul gave the apostles a detailed report of the things God had accomplished through his ministry among the Gentiles. But after listening to him, they began to give him the most demonically engineered advice that he had ever been given. They told Paul that he was a very unpopular figure in the church that was in Jerusalem. They told him that many of the Jews had heard how Paul was teaching the Gentiles not to be circumcised according to Jewish law. Because of this, many Orthodox Jews regarded him as an enemy of Judaism.

> *The apostle Paul was so homesick that he refused to heed the technology of divine interception that God was initiating on his behalf through the prophet Agabus.*

They proceeded to tell Paul that in order to defuse the situation and place himself in a favorable position within the Jewish community, he had to take a purification ceremony in order to renounce the Gospel he had been preaching among the Gentiles. Imagine this; these apostles were asking the apostle Paul to renounce his teachings in the book of Romans, Ephesians and Galatians just to name a few. WOW! Momentarily, Paul became bewitched by his own disobedience to the technology of divine interception and by his own desire to be among his kinsmen.

Paul the Apostle bought into this demonically engineered ploy to denounce the revelation that God had given him about the mystery of Christ and the one new man. He accepted their offer to go into the temple and purify himself after the Law of Moses instead of putting on the "one new man." Halfway through Paul's purification, the Lord decided that He had seen enough foolishness. He was not going to allow Paul to make a mockery of the finished work of Christ in order to fit in with the Jews or the other apostles.

So Paul went to the Temple the next day with the other men. They had already started the purification ritual, so he publicly announced the date when their vows would end and sacrifices would be offered for each of them. [27] The seven days were almost ended when some Jews from the province of Asia saw Paul in the Temple and roused a mob against him. They grabbed him, [28] yelling, "Men of Israel, help us! This is the man who preaches against our people everywhere and tells everybody to disobey the Jewish laws. He speaks against the Temple—and even defiles this holy place by bringing in Gentiles." [29] (For earlier that day they had seen him in the city with Trophimus, a Gentile from Ephesus, and they assumed Paul had taken him into the Temple.) [30] The whole city was rocked by these accusations, and a great riot followed. Paul was grabbed and dragged out of the Temple, and immediately the gates were closed behind him. [31] As they were trying to kill him, word reached the commander of the Roman regiment that all Jerusalem was in an uproar. [32] He immediately called out his soldiers and officers[f] and ran down among the crowd. When the mob saw the commander and the troops coming, they stopped beating Paul. Acts 21:26-32

While Paul was going through the purification process some of the Jews from Asia recognized him. They quickly ran to the Sanhedrin council to report the fact that they had seen Paul desecrating their Temple. When the Council of Jewish religious leaders heard that their most deadly enemy was in town and was desecrating the Temple, they stirred their crowd of zealots against Paul. Soon a crowd of Jewish zealots surrounded the apostle Paul and dragged him out of the Temple.

When the angry mob had dragged Paul out of the Temple they beat him like a punching bag. By the time the Roman centurion arrived to intervene on Paul's behalf, Paul was already a bloody mess. Had the Lord not intervened on Paul's behalf by sending the Roman commander to his rescue, the angry mob would have killed the apostle Paul. The question that quickly comes to mind is this: *"Was this God's will for His servant to be beaten like a dog in public by a mob in the streets of Jerusalem?"* I do not believe for one moment that this was the case. The apostle Paul was simply reaping the rewards of disobeying the technology of divine interception when God initiated it through the prophet Agabus.

If you read Acts chapters 21 to 26, you will see that the apostle Paul went into a long season of divine intervention. He was passed from one courtroom to the next in order to defend himself before the Jews. He lived in a Roman prison cell while he waited to defend himself before the Jews. This passage of Scripture is further proof that it is so much better to yield to the technology of divine interception than to ask God to initiate the technology of divine intervention into our lives.

A HYBRID SCENARIO

"Simon, Simon, Satan has asked to sift each of you like wheat.
[32] But I have pleaded in prayer for you, Simon, that your faith should not fail. So when you have repented and turned to me again, strengthen your brothers." [33] Peter said, "Lord, I am ready to go to prison with you, and even to die with you." [34] But Jesus said, "Peter, let me tell you something. Before the rooster crows tomorrow morning, you will deny three times that you even know me." Luke 22:31-34

Finally, I want to close this chapter by telling you that there are times when God initiates both technologies in our life at the same time. I call this the "hybrid scenario." Luke 22:31-34 is a classic example of this hybrid scenario. Before the Lord Jesus Christ went to the cross he turned to Peter and gave him a very stern warning.

Here is what the Lord Jesus Christ told one of his favorite disciples: *"Simon, Simon, Satan has asked to sift each of you like wheat.*
[32] But I have pleaded in prayer for you, Simon, that your faith should not fail." Utilizing interception technology, the Lord Jesus Christ intercepted a demonic conspiracy to destroy Peter's faith. Jesus prayed against the success of this demonic conspiracy. On the other hand, Luke 22:33-34 deals with divine intervention and not divine interception. Here is what

Jesus said to Peter in verses 33 and 34: *"So when you have repented and turned to me again, strengthen your brothers." ³³ Peter said, "Lord, I am ready to go to prison with you, and even to die with you." ³⁴ But Jesus said, "Peter, let me tell you something. Before the rooster crows tomorrow morning, you will deny three times that you even know me."*

The above passage of Scripture shows us God's purpose for initiating the technology of divine intervention. God showed Peter he was going to deny the Lord three times before the rooster crowed once. This statement by Christ would have been completely devastating had it been the conclusion of the matter. But Jesus assured Peter that God was going to intervene on his behalf so much that when he came through it all he would be in a position of spiritual strength to strengthen many of his brothers and sisters in Christ.

> *By the time the Roman centurion arrived to intervene on Paul's behalf, Paul was already a bloody mess.*

This passage of Scripture shows us that there will be rare moments in our spiritual journey with God when God will initiate the technology of divine intervention, because He wants to show us how capable He is of restoring us and everything we've lost. In certain cases, God will use the technology of divine intervention to show us what has been lost in our lives that we are not even aware of.

LIFE APPLICATION SECTION

MEMORY VERSE

"Then when Jesus came, he found that he had lain in the grave four days already. Now Bethany was night unto Jerusalem, about fifteen furlongs off: And many of the Jews came to Martha and Mary, to comfort them concerning their brother. Then Martha, as soon as she heard that Jesus was coming, went out and met him: but Mary sat still in the house. Then said Martha unto Jesus, Lord, if thou hadst been here, my brother had not died." Luke 11:17-21

REFLECTIONS

What is Divine Interception?

_____

_____

_____

_____

_____

_____

What is Divine Intervention?

_____

_____

_____

_____

_____

_____

JOURNAL YOUR THOUGHTS

INTERCEPTION VERSUS INTERVENTION

CHAPTER EIGHT
THE ANATOMY OF DIVINE INTERCEPTION

In this chapter our investigation into the nomenclature of the spiritual technology of divine interception demands that we surgically analyze the "anatomy of this ancient spiritual technology" that God has made available to all of mankind. To help us delve into the depths of this analysis we must clearly define the science of anatomy.

The online thesaurus dictionary defines the science of anatomy as follows:

1. The bodily structure of a plant or an animal or of any of its parts.

2. The science of the shape and structure of organisms and their parts.

3. A treatise on anatomic science.

4. Dissection of a plant or animal to study the structure, position, and interrelation of its various parts.

5. A skeleton.

6. The human body.

7. A detailed examination or analysis.

Essentially the science of anatomy deals with understanding the internal matrix of any living organism. This science examines the different parts or organs of any living organism and how these individual parts interrelate within the structure of the living organism. Consequently the science of spiritual anatomy, which is a higher and more credible science than the science of natural anatomy, also involves the surgical and spiritual analysis of the internal matrix of any spiritual organism or technology. In our endeavor to understand the technology of divine interception and how we can cooperate with it, it would be prudent of us to understand the "spiritual anatomy" of the technology of divine interception.

In my opinion there are very few scriptural passages that capture the complete anatomy of the technology of divine interception like Genesis 14:17-23. This is why I will use this passage to bring you into a deeper understanding of the spiritual anatomy of the technology of divine interception.

GOD

And Melchizedek, the king of Salem and a priest of God Most High, brought Abram some bread and wine. [19] Melchizedek blessed Abram with this blessing: "Blessed be Abram by God Most High, Creator of heaven and earth. [20] And blessed be God Most High, who has defeated your enemies for you." Then Abram gave Melchizedek a tenth of all the goods he had recovered. Genesis 14:18-20

The first and most important element in the "spiritual anatomy" of the technology of divine interception is "God." *God is the greatest spiritual ingredient of this ancient spiritual technology.* This is why the technology of divine interception is so powerful. This technology is powered by a

God who is all-knowing, all-sufficient and all-powerful. How can such a technology know the realms of failure? How can demonic powers defeat such a powerful spiritual technology? How can anyone who has this technology operating flawlessly in their life or vehicle of commerce ever be defeated?

> *The science of anatomy deals with understanding the internal matrix of any living organism.*

Whichever of the questions above you try to answer, the answer in all instances will be exactly the same: and that is, this technology can never fail! It is completely "fail-proof." Demonic powers are completely powerless in the face of the technology of divine interception. *No vehicle of commerce can ever lose money in any business deal that is undergirded by the technology of divine interception.* Since God in all His might and stature is at the heart of this ancient technology, failure and loss can only exist in a spiritual environment where there is disobedience to this technology by the person(s) God is trying to intercept. The disobedience or ignorance of the person(s) God wants to intercept is the only chance that demonic powers have at defeating this powerful spiritual technology.

When Abram was returning from a victorious campaign after defeating the Babylonian kings, who had captured his nephew Lot when they invaded the country of Sodom, he was intercepted by an eternal King-Priest called Melchizedek. The reason for this divine interception was because the king of Sodom had also heard about Abram's victorious campaign and had left Sodom to meet Abram. The king of Sodom was one of the most wicked kings on earth. He reigned over a community of people who did not believe in any kind of divine morality or common decency. *The king of Sodom had literally sold his soul in the devil's service.* God did not want this wicked king to form a political alliance with Abram.

For more and explicit details about this eternal King-Priest called Melchizedek, please get a copy of my book titled *The Order of Melchizedek*. It is not within the scope of this writing to do a full treatise on this powerful eternal King-Priest. But what I want you to know is that this Melchizedek who "intercepted" Abram on his return from battle is actually an Old Testament manifestation of "Christ" before the virgin birth. We know from the writings of King David and the apostle Paul in the book of Psalms and the book of Hebrews that the "Order of Melchizedek" is the eternal royal priesthood of Christ before He came into the world. This eternal priestly order predates all of creation.

For a child is born to us, a son is given to us. The government will rest on his shoulders. And he will be called: Wonderful Counselor, Mighty God, Everlasting Father, Prince of Peace. Isaiah 9:6

A closer examination of Isaiah 9:6 will clearly show that "Christ" is also "God Most High." Combining the passage from Genesis 14:18-20 and Isaiah 9:6 we can quickly prove that Abram was not intercepted by an earthly priest, but by a divine King-Priest who also happened to be "God Most High." This further proves my argument that God is at the heart of the technology of divine interception whenever this technology manifests on the human plane. This is why this technology can never lead us into failure if we choose to stay in a place of total obedience to God. The technology of divine interception is always INITIATED BY GOD! This is why the technology of divine interception can never be manipulated by demonic powers.

> *The king of Sodom had literally sold his soul in the devil's service. God did not want this wicked king to form a political alliance with Abram.*

THE EVENT OR SUBJECT OF INTERCEPTION

After Abram returned from his victory over Kedorlaomer and all his allies, the king of Sodom went out to meet him in the valley of Shaveh (that is, the King's Valley). Genesis 14:17

The second most important ingredient of the technology of divine interception is the "Event or Subject" of the interception. I have already shown you that the technology of divine interception is always initiated by God, but God only initiates the technology of divine interception around an "event or subject" that shows up on heaven's radar. This "event or subject" always manifests in two forms, namely:

1. The "event or subject" is an important, divinely orchestrated component that can enhance the advancement of the Kingdom of God here on earth.

2. The "event or subject" is a dangerous, demonically engineered component which can hurt God's people or hinder the advancement of the Kingdom of God here on earth.

When the "event or subject" of interception is an "event" the technology of divine interception focuses on the spiritual, social and economic dynamics of the "event" being intercepted. In Abram's case (Gen. 14:17) the "event or subject" of interception was more about the "event" being intercepted than about the "subject" being intercepted. In Abram's case the "event" God was intercepting was an earthly "event" that would have provided the platform for Abram to be seduced into a demonically engineered political alliance with the king of Sodom. The king of Sodom was very aware of the fact that Abram had sold his wife for money in Egypt, so he thought he could bribe Abram into a demonic alliance. I really believe that Melchizedek's interception was the only thing that stood between Abram and certain destruction. In Abram's case the "event" of the interception was a dangerous demonically engineered component which had the potential to hurt Abram or hinder the advancement of the Kingdom of God here on earth.

Let me quickly create a modern day scenario to illustrate what happens when God initiates the technology of divine interception to intercept an "event." Imagine that you are the CEO of KMC Industries, a company that you built from scratch with God's help. One day you drive to your office only to be told by your secretary that there are some high powered investors who want to "buy" your company. You instruct your secretary to bring them into your office. When these high powered venture capitalists enter your office, they tell you that they want to buy your company for twice its present worth. Your emotions start squealing in excitement as you envision a big payday, but your elation lasts for only a few moments, because an "uneasy" feeling begins to rise like a dark cloud over your spirit.

Your logic - driven business mind starts to tell you that you must be crazy to turn down such a lucrative offer, and yet your spirit continues to disagree. What is happening in such a case? More often than not God is trying to intercept an "event" in which a platform exists in which you can underprice your business. Maybe God knows that the offer the venture capitalists gave you was five times less than what your business would be worth if you just held off for twelve more months. The Kingdom of God always suffers damage to its economy whenever Kingdom entrepreneurs "under sell" Kingdom property because they fail to heed the voice of interception.

> *"I know that you live in the city where Satan has his throne, yet you have remained loyal to me. You refused to deny me even when Antipas, my faithful witness, was martyred among you there in Satan's city.[14] "But I have a few complaints against you. You tolerate some among you whose teaching is like that of Balaam, who showed Balak how to trip up the people of Israel. He taught them to sin by eating food offered to idols and by committing sexual sin. [15] In a similar way, you have some Nicolaitans among you who follow the same teaching. [16] Repent of your sin, or I will come to you suddenly and fight against them with the sword of my mouth. Revelation 2:13-16*

When the "event or subject" of interception is a "subject" the technology of divine interception focuses on the spiritual, social and economic impact of the "subject" being intercepted. When the "event or subject" of interception is a "subject" the technology of divine interception focuses on the "teaching, doctrine or philosophy" that God is determined to intercept. By definition "philosophy" is "a system of principles for guidance in practical affairs." God is very interested in the system of principles that His people employ to guide their daily affairs or businesses. If that system of principles has been compromised by "demonic philosophies or the traditions of men" God will always initiate an interception to bring correction to the same.

In the case of Revelation 2:13-16, Jesus Christ was intercepting a very dangerous demonic doctrine that was infusing itself into the life stream of the Church in Pergamum. Jesus Christ called this demonic philosophy "the doctrine of Balaam or the doctrine of the Nicolaitans." Like Balaam of old, the Nicolaitians were teaching early Church believers that they could have an ecumenical, greasy grace attitude toward pagan religious observance and were very liberal in matters of sexual morality. They were great proponents of today's common mantra "after all, 'in this day and age' everybody is doing it" or "I am only human."

The philosophy of the Nicolaitians had such a negative impact on the morality of Kingdom citizens and on the Church's testimony that divine interception became absolutely necessary. This is why Jesus Christ spoke very firmly against the doctrine of the Nicolaitians. From the early '80s to the late '90s Christendom was given a rare treat in the rise of the powerful and Charismatic ministry of legendary speaker and gospel artist Bishop Carlton Pearson. His TV show *Azusa* was viewed by millions around the world. His music ministry was legendary. Bishop Carlton's annual conference in the city of Tulsa attracted many of the elites in Christendom. Conference delegates who either flew or drove into the city of Tulsa were in the thousands. The city of Tulsa pocketed $10-15 million dollars every time Carlton Pearson's *Azusa* conference came to town.

The future of this humorous, dynamic and charismatic figure looked

God is very interested in the system of principles that His people employ to guide their daily affairs or businesses.

very bright. But between the years 2000 and 2004, Bishop Carlton Pearson's mega ministry empire came tumbling down like a deck of cards at a poker game. At the heart of his fall from grace and stardom is a toxic doctrine that Carlton Pearson called the "Gospel of Inclusion." Under this new teaching, Carlton Pearson started teaching his congregation that "every person on earth is already saved; they just do not know it." This teaching is also known as the "doctrine of ultimate reconciliation." The underlying theme in his new teaching was simply this: "all roads lead to God." Great men of God like Dr. Oral Roberts and Bishop TD Jakes tried to intercept this demonic teaching before it destroyed the great ministry that Bishop Pearson had built, but Carlton Pearson refused to accept the technology of divine interception which was coming to him through men and women of God who were part of his inner circle.

Within a couple of years Carlton Pearson's church of 5000 members dwindled to about 200 as the faithful jumped ship. His church and ministry revenues took a swift nose dive. His magnificent church building was foreclosed on while Carlton Pearson was reduced to a mere shadow of what he had once been - one of America's most celebrated spiritual leaders. The greatest victims of Bishop Carlton Pearson's ministerial demise were the faithful in his church who looked up to him. Many of my friends in Tulsa, Oklahoma tell me that many of the faithful who used to attend Carlton Pearson's Higher Dimensions Church, walked away from the Lord in total disillusionment. This is why God always initiates the technology of divine interception whenever a "demonic doctrine" infiltrates the ranks of His Kingdom citizens. Some of these "demonic doctrines" if unchecked can inflict irreparable damage on the spiritual life of God's children and on the advancement of the Kingdom of God here on earth.

Whenever I sense that God has initiated the technology of divine interception in my spirit, I immediately begin to prayerfully search for the "event or subject" that God wants to intercept in my life. I never rest until I have properly discerned or zeroed in on the "event or subject" of interception. This is because I have learned from experience and painfully so, that failure to yield to the technology of divine interception when God initiates it in my life can have disastrous consequences.

"Demonic doctrines" if unchecked can inflict irreparable damage on the spiritual life of God's children and on the advancement of the Kingdom of God here on earth.

THE PERSON (S) BEING INTERCEPTED

After Abram returned from his victory over Kedorlaomer and all his allies, the king of Sodom went out to meet him in the valley of Shaveh (that is, the King's Valley). [18] And Melchizedek, the king of Salem and a priest of God Most High, brought Abram some bread and wine. [19] Melchizedek blessed Abram with this blessing: "Blessed be Abram by God Most High, Creator of heaven and earth. [20] And blessed be God Most High, who has defeated your enemies for you." Then Abram gave Melchizedek a tenth of all the goods he had recovered. Genesis 14:17-20

The third important element of the anatomy of the technology of divine interception involves the "person or persons" being intercepted. Whenever God initiates this ancient spiritual technology there is always a specific "person or persons" that God wants to intercept. This is because God's primary motivation for initiating this powerful spiritual technology is to "deliver" His people from all kinds of demonic or self-entrapments. God does not enjoy seeing His people suffer the consequences of bad choices that could easily be avoided. If natural fathers do not like to see any of their children suffer emotional or financial loss, how much more our loving heavenly Father?

When Melchizedek the eternal King-Priest initiated the technology of divine interception in the King's Valley (Shaveh) Abram was the primary recipient of this divine interception. Melchizedek did not show up on location to intercept Abram's allies; He appeared for Abram's benefit. This is why it is dangerous to try to publicize a personal interception. To my own detriment, I have made the mistake of trying to generalize a personal interception. Whenever I sensed that God had initiated the technology of divine interception in my heart, I would go into a "reasoning process."

This reasoning process went something like this: "God how come they can do it, but I can't?" Thinking that the Lord was treating me unfairly, I reasoned my way into disobedience.

Without fail the results of my disobedience to the technology of divine interception were quite painful. In all cases my disobedience cost me much more than my obedience would have. But why did I try to "publicize" a personal interception? The answer is simple but deeply profound. Since the fall of Adam and Eve (Gen. 3) we all have an inherent desire to transfer the burden of personal obedience onto other people. Adam and Eve both blamed somebody else for their lack of personal obedience to God.

I asked the Lord why He kept initiating the technology of divine interception in my heart, while other Kingdom citizens kept on doing what God would not allow me to do. Here are the reasons He gave me:

- I had a higher calling within the economy of the Kingdom than some of my brothers and sisters in Christ that I was comparing myself to. God showed me that I would influence many more people on earth than the persons that I was comparing myself to.

- I had an "intercept-able or obedient heart" while others didn't.

- The consequences of disobedience to the technology of divine interception are much stiffer for those with higher callings within the economy of the Kingdom.

- Disobedience to the technology of divine interception with the help of other people does not lessen the private pain of corporate disobedience.

After God showed me the above, I began to cooperate with the

My disobedience cost me much more than my obedience would have.

THE SPIRIT OF DIVINE INTERCEPTION

technology of divine interception much more readily. *I have not yet arrived at the place of total obedience to God, but I am striving passionately to live in such a spiritual state.* Without a shadow of a doubt Abram had a higher calling within the economy of the Kingdom than any human being who was alive at the time. Abram was destined to become the father of the Jewish nation and the spiritual father of the New Creation. God was not going to stand by while Abram walked into a demonically engineered plot. God had a big investment in Abram that would have been lost had the king of Sodom succeeded in seducing him into a false political alliance.

"Men," he said, "I believe there is trouble ahead if we go on— shipwreck, loss of cargo, and danger to our lives as well." Acts 27:10

In the case of Acts 27:10 the Holy Spirit was initiating the technology of divine interception through the apostle Paul in order to save both the lives of the persons on the cargo ship, as well as the merchandise on the ship. This passage shows us that there are also cases when God initiates the technology of divine interception in order to deliver a group of people or a vehicle of commerce from impending danger. Unfortunately the owner of the cargo ship (the equivalent of today's CEOs) refused to cooperate with this ancient spiritual technology to the detriment of his corporation. This CEO who refused to yield to the technology of divine interception that God had made available to him through the apostle Paul, suffered great financial loss. He went from prosperity to poverty within a couple of days. What a tragedy.

Acts 27:10 must serve as a clear cut warning to Kingdom entrepreneurs who seem to think that their Law degree or MBA from Harvard or Princeton can sufficiently guide them through the treacherous waters of commerce. This mentality is like a child playing with fire. The corridors of commerce are filled with the skeletons of corporations that once ruled the marketplace before they went bankrupt because of one or a series of bad business deals.

THE PURPOSE BEHIND THE INTERCEPTION

The king of Sodom said to Abram, "Give back my people who were captured. But you may keep for yourself all the goods you have recovered." [22] Abram replied to the king of Sodom, "I solemnly swear to the LORD, God Most High, Creator of heaven and earth, [23] that I will not take so much as a single thread or sandal thong from what belongs to you. Otherwise you might say, 'I am the one who made Abram rich.' Genesis 14:21-23

The fourth and final important element which completes the anatomy of the technology of divine interception is the "Purpose" behind the interception. God never does anything without having a clear cut purpose for what He is doing. Purpose therefore precedes creation. This is why all of God's creation longs to be restored to "Divine Purpose." Dr. Myles Munroe in his bestselling book, *In Pursuit of Purpose,* says that "where purpose is not known abuse is inevitable." If we do not know "God's purpose" behind the interception that He has initiated in our life, we are more likely to disobey His voice in the interception.

Unfortunately, more often than not "God's purpose" for initiating the technology of divine interception in our life or vehicle of commerce is usually hidden, until the "event or subject" of interception has come to pass. In some cases like in Acts 27:10 the purpose of God behind the interception is clearly known. But the most important thing we can learn from the testimony of Scripture is simply this: *"God always has a purpose" behind any interception that He initiates.* We must rest in this important fact, because in many cases God's purpose for the interception will be revealed to us within days, weeks, months or years after the actual interception. In cooperating with the technology of divine interception I have come to discover that "obedience is better than sacrifice."

> *If we do not know "God's purpose" behind the interception that He has initiated in our life, we are more likely to disobey His voice in the interception.*

In the case of Genesis 14:21-23, God's purpose for intercepting Abram was to stop him from making a "demonically engineered" political alliance with the king of Sodom. The king of Sodom had come to present Abram with an offer of money and friendship that he felt Abram could not refuse. The sodomic-demonic system that this king presided over had already destroyed the spiritual life and testimony of Abram's nephew, Lot. Had Abram brought himself under the governing influence of the king of Sodom, God's plan to establish His Kingdom on earth through Abram would have been destroyed. The purpose of God could not have been any clearer. The danger posed by the king of Sodom to Abram's future destiny could not have been any more serious. The threat was real and present; this is why Christ stepped out of eternity in His priestly garments to intercept Abram through the sacrament of Holy Communion.

LIFE APPLICATION SECTION

MEMORY VERSE

For a child is born to us, a son is given to us. The government will rest on his shoulders. And he will be called: Wonderful Counselor, Mighty God, Everlasting Father, Prince of Peace. Isaiah 9:6

REFLECTIONS

Write down the key elements of the anatomy of the Technology of Divine Interception.

_____

_____

_____

_____

_____

_____

Is there a Purpose behind the Technology of Divine Interception?

_____

_____

_____

_____

_____

JOURNAL YOUR THOUGHTS

THE ANATOMY OF DIVINE INTERCEPTION

CHAPTER NINE
PREREQUISITES TO
DIVINE INTERCEPTION

In this chapter we will continue to analyze the technology of divine interception but we will shift our focus to the "prerequisites" for this powerful ancient spiritual technology. By definition the word "prerequisite" carries the following meaning: "something which is required or necessary as a prior condition; for instance, competence is prerequisite to promotion." In this chapter we will analyze important "prerequisites" that serve as spiritual catalysts in the rapid manifestation of the technology of divine interception. Stated simply, these prerequisites collectively create a "spiritual climate" that is completely conducive for the manifestation of the technology of divine interception.

LEAN NOT ON YOUR OWN UNDERSTANDING

Trust in the LORD with all your heart; do not depend on your own understanding. ⁶ Seek his will in all you do, and he will show you which path to take. Proverbs 3:5-6

King Solomon, the wisest man who has ever lived, starts us off with one of the prerequisites to the technology of divine interception. Solomon admonishes every living person on earth, especially Kingdom citizens, not to "lean on our own human understanding of things." Without a shadow of a doubt our fallen nature worships itself. Hell is full of people, both rich and poor, who are serving their eternal sentence because while they were on earth they refused to give up their perspective on life to gain God's perspective. They worshipped their own opinions and placed them above the written word of God.

This inherent human tendency to worship our own "opinion" or "lean on our own understanding" is both common and universal. I am sure King Solomon during his tenure as the king over Israel saw many people or businessmen who destroyed their future because they leaned too heavily on their own limited perspective of life. In Proverbs 3:5-6 the wisest and richest man who has ever lived admonishes us not to lean on our own understanding, but to acknowledge God's eternal perspective in all our business dealings.

King Solomon concludes his timeless warning with a very powerful but timeless promise. He guarantees us "divine interception" or "divine intervention" in all the affairs of our lives or business if we simply acknowledge God in all that we do. Kingdom entrepreneurs who abide by this timeless prerequisite will always excite the engines of either "divine interception" or "divine intervention" in their vehicles of commerce. The technology of divine interception is always enhanced in any spiritual atmosphere where the person(s) being intercepted acknowledges God in all their ways.

ACKNOWLEDGE THE POWER OF THE TITHE

After Abram returned from his victory over Kedorlaomer and all his allies, the king of Sodom went out to meet him in the valley of Shaveh (that is, the King's Valley). [18] And Melchizedek, the king of Salem and a priest of God Most High, brought Abram some bread and wine. [19] Melchizedek blessed Abram with this blessing: "Blessed be Abram by God Most High, Creator of heaven and earth.[20] And blessed be God Most High, who has defeated your enemies for you." Then Abram gave Melchizedek a tenth of all the goods he had recovered. Genesis 14:17-20

Without a doubt one of the most powerful Scripture passages that exposes the inner and outer workings of the technology of divine interception is Genesis 14:17-22. This passage contains the anatomy of the technology of divine interception, but it also contains one important prerequisite which greatly accelerates the manifestation of this spiritual technology. This prerequisite in my opinion is probably one of the most important prerequisites for cooperating with the technology of divine interception.

> *This inherent human tendency to worship our own "opinion" or "lean on our own understanding" is both common and universal.*

This "prerequisite" is the "power of the tithe." When Melchizedek (Christ) appeared to Abram in the Valley of Shaveh (Gen. 14) in order to intercept the demonic machinery which was headed toward Abram through the king of Sodom, He came with "bread and wine." I have dedicated a whole chapter in my book, *The Order of Melchizedek,* to describe the spiritual technology behind the heavenly "bread and wine" that this eternal King-Priest gave to Abram. But it suffices to say that these spiritual elements were critical components in the "mechanics" of manifesting the technology of divine interception in Abram's life.

Melchizedek, the King-Priest, came on location to bring Abram into a living covenant with God. It is common knowledge that all covenants always involve two or more persons. It is also understood that "covenant" is never a one-sided deal. Each side of the covenant agreement is required by covenant law to bring something of "equitable" value to the covenant. In the "covenant of interception" which Melchizedek established with Abram, the eternal King-Priest brought heavenly "bread and wine" to the covenant.

The million dollar question that we need to ask ourselves is simply this: *"What did Abram (who was representing all of humanity in this spiritual transaction) bring to the covenant of interception?"* The answer stares us in the face when we examine Genesis 14:20. Abram gave Melchizedek "tithes of all." He gave this eternal King-Priest "tithes of honor." A tithe is a tenth of all he had. The Church's obsession with the Malachi 3 tithing model has unfortunately masked the "real power" of the tithe. By teaching that the primary purpose of the "tithe" is to "acquire" more money, the Church has undermined one of the most important "prerequisites" to manifesting the technology of divine interception.

The "real power" of the "tithe" lies in its ability to act as a "covenant catalyst" in the process of accelerating the manifestation of one of the greatest spiritual technologies in all of creation. This spiritual technology is the technology of divine interception. Kingdom citizens who do not "tithe" are making a grave and dangerous mistake. Kingdom citizens who do not "tithe" are in essence telling God and demonic powers that they do not care about the technology of divine interception. How can we call ourselves the "seed of Abraham" (Gal. 3) while refusing to emulate his example in the area of tithing? Millions of dollars in Kingdom resources are stolen by the devil every year, because many Kingdom citizens and entrepreneurs are not participating in sowing "tithes of honor." Therefore much is being lost to the enemy because of the absence of a functional technology of divine interception.

CHOOSE OBEDIENCE WITHOUT QUESTION

But Samuel replied, "What is more pleasing to the LORD: your burnt offerings and sacrifices or your obedience to his voice? Listen! Obedience is better than sacrifice, and submission is better than offering the fat of rams. 1 Samuel 15:22

And thine ears shall hear a word behind thee, saying, This is the way, walk ye in it, when ye turn to the right hand, and when ye turn to the left. Isaiah 30:21 KJV

There is nothing on the human plane that God "honors" more than "obedience." There are those who would say that "faith" is the main thing. But I opt to disagree. "Faith" finds its relevance in the "canals of obedience." Genuine biblical "faith" is "rooted in obedience" to God. Faith without obedience is nothing less than "foolish assumption" and many Kingdom citizens who have tried to have faith without obedience have brought great sorrow into their lives. The apostle Paul would say that they have "made shipwreck" of their faith.

Without any hesitation I want to emphasize that "obedience" to God is one of the primary "prerequisites" to manifesting the technology of divine interception. Without obedience Kingdom citizens and entrepreneurs will not heed the "warning sirens" that God has placed on the highway of divine interception. I have talked to many Kingdom entrepreneurs who told me that had they listened to the prompting of the Holy Spirit, they would not have lost millions of dollars in a business deal God knew was destined to fail miserably.

I remember a couple of years ago, when the Holy Spirit gave me a prophetic warning for a certain Kingdom entrepreneur. He was about to relocate the headquarters of his company to another U.S. city. I told him that the Lord said that he was not to do this because the move would excite a "chain of demonically engineered events" that would hurt his company and his family. He did not listen to my prophetic counsel. He was advised by his new business partners that the move to this city made a lot of business sense. Within eighteen months of moving to this new city, he lost all the "proposed investment" money that his new business partners had promised him. The relationship between this Kingdom entrepreneur and his new business partners quickly went sour. The stress of this whole transition placed a heavy toll on this Kingdom entrepreneur's family and created some irreparable damage.

This is why I am so passionate about emphasizing the importance of "obedience" as one of the key prerequisites for manifesting the technology of divine interception. Everything that I have written in this book will not bring you any kind of profit if you do not have a "heart of obedience." In the absence of a "heart of obedience" this book will simply join many other books on your bookshelf that you bought but never read or implemented. King Saul lost his right to the throne of Israel because his lack of obedience "nullified" the technology of divine interception that God had made available to him. God actually compares "disobedience" to the "spirit of witchcraft." I really believe that it is "obedience" which gives "substance" to our faith.

> The "real power" of the "tithe" lies in its ability to act as a "covenant catalyst" in the process of accelerating the manifestation of one of the greatest spiritual technologies in all of creation.

DEVELOP SENSITIVITY TO THE VOICE OF GOD

"Go out and stand before me on the mountain," the LORD told him. And as Elijah stood there, the LORD passed by, and a mighty windstorm hit the mountain. It was such a terrible blast that the rocks were torn loose, but the LORD was not in the wind. After the wind there was an earthquake, but the LORD was not in the earthquake. [12] And after the earthquake there was a fire, but the LORD was not in the fire. And after the fire there was the sound of a gentle whisper. [13] When Elijah heard it, he wrapped his face in his cloak and went out and stood at the entrance of the cave. And a voice said, "What are you doing here, Elijah?" 1 Kings 19:11-13

I have never heard of a baby who was born talking. But how are most mothers able to accurately distinguish the meaning between the different cries that the baby makes? They know when the baby is crying because it wants to eat and when the baby is crying because it's hungry. Many mothers are able to wake up from a deep sleep and instantly know the baby is not feeling well. How can we explain this phenomenon? Most mothers tell me that this is due to an acquired sensitivity to the baby's needs that most mothers develop while the baby is in the womb.

I really believe that it behooves us as citizens of the Kingdom of God to develop the art of hearing God's voice. Hearing God's voice is not difficult but it takes practice and unwavering determination. Like mothers who are nursing infants we must begin to train and "sensitize" all our spiritual faculties so that we can easily discern the voice of God. More often than not God will speak to us in a "gentle whisper" as opposed to an audible voice. One of the key prerequisites for manifesting the technology of divine interception is being "sensitive" to the voice of God.

Whenever I counsel married couples the number one request that wives make of their husbands involves the issue of "sensitivity." In 1 Kings 19:11-13 God uses the prophet Elijah to showcase the vital role that "sensitivity to the voice of God" plays in the manifestation of the technology of divine interception. All movie goers appreciate movies that are loaded with special effects. God had special effects of His own that he tested the prophet Elijah on. The first special divine effect came in the form of a powerful mountain shaking "windstorm." The second came in the form of a great "earthquake" which caused the foundations of the earth to rattle. The third one came in the form of a "supernatural bowl of fire." The prophet Elijah was not moved by either of these dazzling special effects, because he discerned that the Lord's presence was not in any of them. God's power was behind the special effects but His presence was not in them.

Finally God spoke to Elijah in a "gentle whisper." By definition to "whisper" is "to speak with soft, hushed sounds, using the breath, lips, etc., but with no vibration of the vocal cords." God spoke so softly that had the prophet Elijah not developed heightened sensitivity to the voice of God, he would have missed the voice of interception. He would have left the mountain of God without clear instructions about his future destiny. This is why I am convinced that "sensitivity" to the voice of God is an important prerequisite to manifesting the technology of divine interception.

DENOUNCE PRIDE AND EMBRACE HUMILITY

But he gives us even more grace to stand against such evil desires. As the Scriptures say, "God opposes the proud but favors the humble."[7] So humble yourselves before God. Resist the devil, and he will flee from you. James 4:6-7

Pride goes before destruction, and haughtiness before a fall.

THE ANATOMY OF DIVINE INTERCEPTION

Proverbs 16:18

The corridors of human history are plastered with the stories of great men and women who fell from their positions of grandeur because they failed to "embrace humility." They allowed "pride" to eat them up. It is common knowledge that having immeasurable wealth, fame and power can easily inflame the engines of pride that are embedded within the core of our fallen nature.

Pride is such an enemy of God that God promises in James 4:6-7 that He will always "resist or contend with" those who are full of pride. How can we expect the technology of divine interception to operate seamlessly in a spiritual climate that is governed by the spirit of pride? Proverbs 16:18 tells us that "pride" always comes before "destruction." This means that a prideful person will easily ignore all the "roadblocks" that God has set in place to intercept demonic technologies. This is why I am convinced that denouncing pride while embracing humility is one of the key prerequisites for cooperating with the technology of divine interception.

While God is an enemy of pride, He quickly makes Himself an ally of those who choose to humble themselves before Him. When the prophet Jonah preached a message of fire and brimstone and impending destruction to the people of Nineveh, the king of Nineveh and his people humbled themselves before God. The king called a nationwide fast of sackcloth and ashes which extended even to their animals. As a result of this king's humility, Jonah's proclamation of impending disaster against this ancient city was suspended. Kingdom entrepreneurs who desire to see the technology of divine interception become a functional spiritual technology in their life and vehicle of commerce must choose to "embrace humility while renouncing pride."

> *Like mothers who are nursing infants we must begin to train and "sensitize" all our spiritual faculties so that we can easily discern the voice of God.*

GET RID OF UNFORGIVENESS OR BITTERNESS

And his lord was wroth, and delivered him to the tormentors, till he should pay all that was due unto him. [35]So likewise shall my heavenly Father do also unto you, if ye from your hearts forgive not every one his brother their trespasses. Matthew 18:34-35 KJV

Since the fall of Adam and Eve, the first Kingdom ambassadors, life on Earth has been plagued by ongoing cycles of both avoidable and unavoidable suffering. Some of these pain-causing demonic cycles revolve around interpersonal relationships. When God walked into the Garden of Eden after Adam and Eve committed high treason, the game of blame shifting started; this showcased the fracture that sin had embedded into the internal matrix of human relationships. Adam blamed his wife for his failure to obey God and she blamed the serpent for her failure to obey God. Neither of them took responsibility for their own actions.

It does not take the mind of a rocket scientist to quickly conclude that in an environment compromised by sin and man's inherent self-centeredness, the probability of people hurting or taking advantage of each other is quite high. It is very easy for us to hold a grudge against people who have hurt or taken advantage of us. This is why life is full of opportunities for us to live in unforgiveness. If we refuse to forgive people of the wrongs they have committed against us we nullify the manifestation of the technology of divine interception.

The Scriptures are clear that God's power does not operate in an atmosphere of unforgiveness. Jesus said that when we do not forgive those who have wronged us, God will hand us over to the "tormentors" (demonic powers.) This is why I hate to nurse feelings of unforgiveness. I treasure the technology of divine interception to such an extent that I will not allow unforgiveness to shut down the operation of this important technology in my life. If we allow unforgiveness to nest in our hearts for a long time, it turns into "bitterness." Bitterness is the terminal cancer of the soul. It completely camouflages its victim's personality in a "demonic exterior," while completely poisoning the heart. It is my experience that it is very difficult for people who are bitter to yield to the technology of divine interception when it manifests itself to them. This is why getting rid of "unforgiveness and bitterness" is one of the key prerequisites for cooperating with the technology of divine interception.

SEEK THE COUNSEL OF WISE LEADERS

Plans go wrong for lack of advice; many advisers bring success. Proverbs 15:22

So don't go to war without wise guidance; victory depends on having many advisers. Proverbs 24:6

In my humble opinion one of the quickest ways to engage the technology of divine interception is to seek the "counsel" of godly leaders or Kingdom entrepreneurs. I really believe that "seeking the Counsel" of wise leaders who can give the advantage of "hind-sight, in-sight and fore-sight" in any business endeavor that we are venturing into, is wisdom. This is why "seeking the counsel of wise leaders" is an important prerequisite for cooperating with the technology of divine interception.

In Proverbs 15:22 and 24:6, King Solomon shows us why "consulting" with wise and godly leaders is important to Kingdom entrepreneurs who desire to win big in life and business. Below are some bullet points from the writings of King Solomon that underscore why "seeking the counsel" of wise leaders is a critical prerequisite for cooperating with the technology of divine interception.

- Plans (including business plans) go wrong for lack of advice

- Consulting many advisers (experts within their field of business) can bring success

- It is dangerous to go to war with limited intelligence

- Victory (in life and business) depends on having many advisers

DO NOT WORSHIP YOUR EGO

"Why are you so angry?" the LORD asked Cain. "Why do you look so dejected? [7] *You will be accepted if you do what is right. But if you refuse to do what is right, then watch out! Sin is crouching at the door, eager to control you. But you must subdue it and be its master." Genesis 4:6-7*

Among the many prerequisites to manifesting the technology of divine interception that we have thus far analyzed, perhaps none can compete with the disruptive impact that "ego" has on our ability to effectively cooperate with the technology of divine interception. I have never met a human being who has mastered their ego apart from Christ. Ego is the disease of the soul which affects every human being. This spiritual disease is the direct consequence of Adam and Eve's fall from grace. By definition "ego" commands the following meaning: "EGO" is the "I" or self of any person; a person as thinking, feeling, and willing, and distinguishing itself from the selves of others and from objects of its thought. EGO as an acronym stands for Edging God Out.

In an atmosphere of sinless perfection, being driven by "ego" would not pose a real threat, because everyone's "ego" would be tempered and controlled by Christ-likeness. But this is not the reality you and I must live in. The fall of Adam and Eve created a "perverted or demonically engineered" view of self in relation to others. Since this catastrophic fall of the first Kingdom ambassadors, mankind's "ego" is now deeply rooted in "self-centeredness and self-preservation."

> *I have never met a human being who has mastered their ego apart from Christ. Ego is the disease of the soul, which affects every human being.*

When God saw that the "entity or principle" called "Sin" was crouching like a starving tiger ready to pounce on Cain, God initiated the technology of divine interception. Cain was very offended with God. He was upset because God had accepted his young brother's sacrifice while He rejected his. Cain's offense was beginning to spill over into very dangerous territory. God told Cain that if he did not handle his offense properly "Sin" would have the best of him. Just reading the text would show even the dumbest among us, that God was initiating divine interception. But it was up to Cain to accept or reject the technology of divine interception.

Cain had an opportunity to disappoint the demonic powers that were baiting him to ignore the technology of divine interception. But Cain forfeited this golden opportunity because he had a "Huge Ego." His ego could not bring him to accept the fact that his younger brother (Abel) had discovered a better technology for accessing the presence of God than he did. People with huge egos have a difficult time accepting defeat or the counsel of others. How much would you pay to have God as your chief legal counsel when you are facing the legal battle of your lifetime? But Cain's ego would not let him listen to the counsel of He "who sees the end from the beginning." Cain's ego turned him into the first murderer on earth. He was banished from God's manifest presence and he became a spiritual vagabond. This is why I am a firm believer that "refusing to worship our own ego" is one of the most important prerequisites to cooperating with the technology of divine interception

Without a doubt millions if not billions of dollars in Kingdom resources are "wasted" or "plundered" by the enemy at the altar of human ego. When God created the first humans He inscribed the spirit of "dominion" into their DNA so they could effortlessly subdue the earth on behalf of the Kingdom of Heaven. But then after the fall the ground was cursed. Kingdom entrepreneurs and church leaders must not mistake the "spirit of dominion" for "ego." The former is divine while the latter is devilish and counter productive. I have talked to marketplace leaders who told me that they would not have lost thousands of dollars in financial resources had they listened to counsel of their wives. I asked them to tell me why they did not listen to their wives, and in most cases their "ego" would not let them submit to their wife's godly counsel.

GET OVER THE FEAR OF MAN

Fearing people is a dangerous trap, but trusting the LORD means safety. Proverbs 29:25

One of the most dangerous demonic technologies that is in operation in the earth realm is called "FEAR." The demonic technology behind this four-letter word is responsible for much of the suffering that plagues our world. Some biblical scholars have defined FEAR as "False Evidence Appearing Real." I love this definition of fear because it captures the capstone of this demonic technology. What is this? All FEAR is based upon a "False" perception of God and His creation. All FEAR is based upon a "False" illusion of reality.

FEAR was one of the first demonic technologies to manifest itself immediately after the fall of Adam and Eve. When the first ambassadorial couple heard the voice of God walking in the Garden of Eden in the cool of the day, they were afraid and hid themselves from the presence of God. This fear was also mixed with shame because of their disobedience and nakedness. It is important to distinguish between healthy (godly) and unhealthy (demonic) fear. Scripture says that the fear of the Lord is the beginning of knowledge and wisdom. (Prov. 1:7, 9:10)

Another of the greatest and most common FEARS is the "fear of man." King Solomon eludes to the danger of this demonically engineered fear in Proverbs 29:25. King Solomon tells us that the "fear of man" will always ensnare and lead us out of the covenant of total obedience to God. The fear of man is really rooted in our deep-seated fear of rejection. Many Kingdom citizens are not yet rooted in Christ's acceptance of them, so they shy away from saying or doing things that might cause their peers to reject them. In the marketplace the above scenario is very common, especially in the political arena where toeing the "party line" is expected of all party representatives. Sometimes this causes born again politicians to keep silent at a time when God wants them to speak up. Had it not been for Mordecai's steadfast leadership, Queen Esther would have ignored and forfeited the technology of divine interception that God was initiating through her to save the Jewish people from global annihilation.

> *Mordecai sent this reply to Esther: "Don't think for a moment that because you're in the palace you will escape when all other Jews are killed. [14] If you keep quiet at a time like this, deliverance and relief for the Jews will arise from some other place, but you and your relatives will die. Who knows if perhaps you were made queen for just such a time as this?" Esther 4:13-14*

Queen Esther, or Haddasah as she was known to her people, almost made the tragic mistake of "fearing man" more than God in a critical time of interception. When Mordecai instructed her to come before her king-husband to intercede for the fate of her people, she was terrified of what the king or his armed guards would do to her if she approached the king without being invited by the same. She rehearsed all her fears to Mordecai hoping to secure his sympathy. But Mordecai reminded her that her silence and residency in the royal palace would not save her from Haman's evil decree, because Haman's decree targeted every person of Jewish descent despite their nobility. Mordecai's censure helped Esther break free of her "fear of man" in order to cooperate with the technology of divine interception. The rest is history.

Tommy Tenney's movie, *One Night with the King,* produced by Gener8Xion Entertainment and TBN films, would never have happened had Esther failed to break free of the demonic technology called the "fear of man." As I mentioned earlier, a dear friend of mine told me the story of how she lost a 17 million dollar company that she and her dad took public, because she allowed the "fear of man" to silence her in the midst of a merger with another business partner. Two years later my friend and her dad lost the company they started from scratch to their new business partner. The loss of their company was devastating and catastrophic. This is why I am convinced that "breaking free" of the "fear of man" is one of the most important prerequisites to cooperating with the technology of divine interception.

DO NOT ABUSE YOUR SPOUSE

In the same way, you husbands must give honor to your wives. Treat your wife with understanding as you live together. She may be weaker than you are, but she is your equal partner in God's gift of new life. Treat her as you should so your prayers will not be hindered. 1 Peter 3:7

In my humble opinion this final prerequisite that we are about to analyze is responsible for why many instances of divine interception were forfeited by those whom God was wanting to intercept. This final prerequisite literally brings the technology of divine interception right into our homes and only applies to Kingdom citizens and entrepreneurs who are married. If you are currently single but desire to get married in the future, this prerequisite is one that you need to understand before you tie the knot.

In 1 Peter 3:7 the apostle Peter admonishes all born-again husbands to live with their wives (spouse) according to knowledge. Husbands who are Kingdom citizens are admonished to "honor" their wives and treat them with great tenderness, because they are fellow heirs of the "grace of life." The apostle Peter goes further and states that failure by husbands in this arena would "hinder" their prayers for "divine interception." This is truly serious and yet this is the area that many born-again husbands are failing in. I can honestly say that some opportunities for divine interception that I missed, happened at a time when my wife and I were operating in strife toward each other. Currently we rarely go to bed with any unresolved conflict. Both my wife and I have come to seriously treasure the technology of divine interception. We do not want to stand in the way of this powerful technology. We want it to be working in our favor constantly.

I truly believe that multiple millions of dollars and time are wasted each year globally because of Kingdom entrepreneurs and pastors who have not yet mastered 1 Peter 3:7. Many moments of divine interception failed to initiate because of ongoing "strife and abuse" between husbands and wives within the Kingdom economy. This is why I am convinced that choosing not to "dishonor or abuse" your spouse is one of the key prerequisites for cooperating with the technology of divine interception. The technology of divine interception does not operate effectively in a spiritual climate that is driven by the engines of strife between husband and wife. It works better in a spiritual environment that is driven by the eternal engines of God's peace. This is why Paul the Apostle admonished all Kingdom citizens to allow the "peace of Christ" to rule in their hearts.

CULTIVATE AN ATMOSPHERE OF AGREEMENT?

I also tell you this: If two of you agree here on earth concerning anything you ask, my Father in heaven will do it for you. Matthew 18:19

For where envying and strife is, there is confusion and every evil work. James 3:16

As I mentioned at the beginning of this book, this book is about a very powerful spiritual technology – the technology of divine interception. But all technologies whether they are natural or spiritual function around a set system of protocols. Violating any one of the necessary protocols diminishes the operational capacity of any technology. This principle also applies to the technology of divine interception. One of those important spiritual protocols that facilitates and accelerates the technology of divine interception is "an atmosphere of agreement." This is one of the most important prerequisites for cooperating with the technology of divine interception. The lack of an atmosphere of agreement is reason why the technology of divine interception is hindered in many marriages, businesses and churches.

James the Apostle tells us that wherever there is "envy and strife" there is confusion and every evil work. This means that in the absence of an atmosphere of agreement you have "envy and strife" which is the breeding ground for all sorts of demonic technologies. This is one of the reasons why we are admonished by Scripture "not to let the sun go down on our wrath."

LIFE APPLICATION SECTION

MEMORY VERSE

Trust in the LORD with all your heart; do not depend on your own understanding. [6] Seek his will in all you do, and he will show you which path to take. Proverbs 3:5-6

REFLECTIONS

What is a prerequisite?

_____

_____

_____

_____

_____

_____

Write down three prerequisites of the Technology of Divine Interception?

_____

_____

_____

_____

_____

_____

THE ANATOMY OF DIVINE INTERCEPTION

JOURNAL YOUR THOUGHTS

CHAPTER TEN
THE MECHANICS OF THE TECHNOLOGY
OF DIVINE INTERCEPTION

In this chapter we will now focus our attention on understanding the mechanics of the technology of divine interception. By definition, the mechanics of any technology deals with "the functional and technical aspects of an activity." So we will now examine the functional and technical aspects of the technology of divine interception. The mechanics of any activity usually involves understanding the nuts and bolts of the technology or mechanism that is being examined. In this case, we will be examining the nuts and bolts of the technology of divine interception.

THE GODHEAD

In the beginning the Word already existed. The Word was with God, and the Word was God.²He existed in the beginning with God.³ God created everything through him, and nothing was created except through him. John 1:1-3

THE MECHANICS OF THE TECHNOLOGY OF DIVINE INTERCEPTION

Several days later a man named Agabus, who also had the gift of prophecy, arrived from Judea. ¹¹ He came over, took Paul's belt, and bound his own feet and hands with it. Then he said, "The Holy Spirit declares, 'So shall the owner of this belt be bound by the Jewish leaders in Jerusalem and turned over to the Gentiles.'" Acts 21:10-11

The first and most important mechanism of the technology of divine interception is the Godhead. Without the involvement of the Godhead the technology of divine interception loses its functionality. In John chapter 1:1-3 the Bible tells us that "In the beginning God…" This foundational expression underscores why the technology of divine interception is so powerful. It is powerful because it begins with God in its mechanics. Nothing can fail or suffer defeat if it begins with God, because God knows the end from the beginning.

Since God created everything in nature, there is nothing that He cannot intercept and overturn. When the prophet Agabus prophesied over the apostle Paul and warned him against going to Jerusalem, the Holy Spirit was very much a part of this interception. In this case, the Holy Spirit was an intricate part of the mechanism that God put in place to intercept Paul. We can never fully operate in the technology of divine interception if we do not appreciate the fact that the Godhead is the most important part of the mechanism of this ancient technology.

KAIROS TIME

To every thing there is a season, and a time to every purpose under the heaven: Ecclesiastes 3:1 KJV

The second most important element, which is an intricate part of the mechanics of the technology of divine interception, is "Kairos time." It is important for us to understand this very important element because misunderstanding this element can cause us to miss out on prophetic moments pregnant with the technology of divine interception. There are two time zones that are revealed to us in the Holy Scriptures. These two time zones describe two distinct and independent time frames.

The first time zone is a natural time zone governed by the physical laws of nature. In the Greek this natural time zone is known as "Chronos." This is where we get the English derivative "chronology." By definition the word "chronology" refers to "the science of arranging time in periods and ascertaining the dates and historical order of past events." This means that all natural calendars are the sequential arrangement of natural time frames. There is nothing supernatural about "Chronos" because it is governed by the physical laws of nature. Our calendar days Monday, Tuesday, Wednesday and so forth are based upon "Chronos," as well as the timeline distinctions known as B.C. and A.D., where Christ is the demarcation line of history.

> *Since God created everything in nature, there is nothing that He cannot intercept and overturn.*

We appreciate "Chronos," because without it we would have no way of knowing what time it is at any given moment; without "Chronos," we could never be able to celebrate special days like birthdays and anniversaries. Having said so, there is a higher and loftier timeframe than "Chronos." This second time zone is a spiritual time zone that is governed by the laws of the spirit world. In the Greek, this second time zone is known as "Kairos." "Kairos" is a prophetic time zone where the supernatural intersects or intercepts "Chronos."

> *Now there is at Jerusalem by the sheep market a pool, which is called in the Hebrew tongue Bethesda, having five porches. ³In these lay a great multitude of impotent folk, of blind, halt, withered, waiting for the moving of the water. ⁴For an angel went down at a certain season into the pool, and troubled the water: whosoever then first after the troubling of the water stepped in was made whole of whatsoever disease he had. John 5:2-4 KJV*

In moments of "Kairos" there is a supernatural stirring of the water on the natural flow of things. The Gospel of John contains one of the most graphic examples of the difference between "Chronos" and "Kairos." The Bible says that there was a pool in Bethesda which had five porches.

THE MECHANICS OF THE TECHNOLOGY OF DIVINE INTERCEPTION

This pool was like a hospital of a great multitude of diseased people. The Bible tells us that periodically an angel of God would come and step into the water of the pool. When the angel of God stepped into the water, the healing power of God was released into the water at that specific moment. Whosoever was first to jump into the water after the angel had stirred the water was instantly healed. The action of the angel stirring the water created a portal of divine interception in the water.

What we need to understand from this prophetic story about the nature of "Kairos" is that it is beyond human manipulation. No human being can create a moment of "Kairos." This prophetic moment of interception can only be created by God himself. Why is this important for us to understand? It is important for us to understand this because if we fail to respond to the technology of divine interception within a specified moment of "Kairos," we will miss God and schedule disaster in our future.

> *In moments of "Kairos" there is a supernatural stirring of the water which affects the natural flow of things.*

Please remember that God does not operate on our time schedule. God almighty is too lofty to be controlled by man's timetable. Please remember that God created time, but does not live in it nor is constrained by it. But when God creates a special moment of time to intercept a demonic and diabolical assignment against us, it would be prudent of us to respond to Him immediately. If we are going to become masters at cooperating with the technology of divine interception, we must understand that this spiritual technology operates within the context of God's timing. This is why King Solomon tells us that *God makes all things beautiful in His time.*

If God initiates the technology of divine interception and tells us to sell off all our shares in a particular stock, we must do it immediately. Failure to do so could have disastrous consequences because the technology of divine interception is always time sensitive. I know many Kingdom citizens who are now going through divine intervention because they failed to respond to the technology of divine interception in a time sensitive manner. By the time they decided to come into a place of obedience to the technology of divine interception, the moment of "Kairos" had come and gone and it was too late. They missed their day or hour of visitation.

> *For the days shall come upon thee, that thine enemies shall cast a trench about thee, and compass thee round, and keep thee in on every side, [44]And shall lay thee even with the ground, and thy children within thee; and they shall not leave in thee one stone upon another; because thou knewest not the time of thy visitation. Luke 19:43-44 KJV*

The above passage of Scripture is probably one of the saddest passages in the Gospels. I can almost feel the sadness that was in Jesus' heart when He said this to his covenant people. Jesus knew that salvation was of the Jews first and then the Gentiles. But the people of Israel had religiously rejected their promised Messiah. Said simply, they had rejected their time of visitation. Being a prophet of God, Jesus looked into the future destiny of the people of Israel, and saw the vicious attack that they would suffer at the hands of the Romans. Jesus could see the spiritual ramifications of missing this divine moment of divine interception, and He wept for Israel.

BREAD AND WINE

> *After Abram returned from his victory over Kedorlaomer and all his allies, the king of Sodom went out to meet him in the valley of Shaveh (that is, the King's Valley). And Melchizedek, the king of Salem and a priest of God Most High, brought Abram some bread and wine. Melchizedek blessed Abram with this blessing: "Blessed be Abram by God Most High, Creator of heaven and earth. And blessed be God Most High, who has defeated your enemies for you." Then Abram gave Melchizedek a tenth of all the goods he had recovered. Genesis 14:17-20*

The above Scripture passage says that there was a divine covenant exchange that took place between Abram and Melchizedek, the eternal King-Priest. Melchizedek gave Abram bread and wine *and Abram gave Him tithes of honor.* Let us examine the prophetic implications of the sacred bread and wine that Abram was given by Melchizedek. Incidentally, this bread and wine make up the third most important element of the technology of divine interception. It is one of the key mechanisms for the proper functioning and operation of divine interception.

> *And Melchizedek, the king of Salem and a priest of God Most High, brought Abram some bread and wine.*

In the Bible there are several prophetic representations of the sacred bread that Melchizedek gave to Abram. By examining these prophetic representations we quickly come to terms with the critical importance of the sacred bread and its vital role in *manifesting the technology of divine interception on the human plane.* Bread in the Bible symbolizes the following prophetic dimensions.

1. The Doctrine of the Kingdom of God

*Jesus also used this illustration: "The Kingdom of Heaven is like the yeast a woman used her in making **bread** (emphasis added). Even though she put only a little yeast in three measures of flour, it permeated every part of the dough." Matthew 13:3.*

Many churches today are out of touch with Jesus Christ's primary message. I believe that the global Church's obsession with the idea of going to heaven has robbed it of the primary passion and mission of Jesus Christ. What is adamantly clear when we examine the message and ministry of Jesus is that He was never obsessed with the idea of getting people to heaven. *His primary message was about restoring the reality and influence of the Kingdom of heaven here on earth.*

Contrary to what many so-called Christians believe, God created man to live here on earth. God never created humankind for the ultimate purpose of transferring his residence from the earth to heaven. The truth of the matter is that if Adam and Eve had never sinned, there would have been no need for anyone to go to heaven. Heaven only became God's temporary transition home for His people after Adam's sin introduced death to the planet Earth.

*Seek the **Kingdom** (emphasis added) of God above all else, and live righteously, and he will give you everything you need. Matthew 6:33*

2. Deliverance from Demonic Oppression

*And behold, a woman of Canaan came from that region and cried out to Him, saying, "Have mercy on me, O Lord, Son of David! My daughter is severely demon-possessed." But He answered her not a word. And His disciples came and urged Him, saying, "Send her away, for she cries out after us." But He answered and said, "I was not sent except to the lost sheep of the house of Israel." Then she came and worshiped Him, saying, "Lord, help me!" But He answered and said, "It is not good to take the **children's bread** (emphasis added) and throw it to the little dogs." And she said, "Yes, Lord, yet even the little dogs eat the crumbs which fall from their masters' table." Matthew 15:22-27 NKJV*

Ever since Adam and Eve's messy encounter with the devil in the Garden of Eden, the warfare between mankind and demons has only escalated. What is clear from observing this demons-against-humankind warfare is that the devil hates humankind with an unimaginable passion because we were created in the image of God and the devil hates God.

The widespread demonic oppression of the masses by demonic powers is evidence of this ongoing warfare between the Kingdom of Light and the kingdom of darkness. Cases of mental, emotional, and physical oppression have reached an all-time high. Both Christians and Kingdom citizens are not completely immune to these subversive attacks of the enemy if they do not know how to release the power of God to intercept the same.

When the Canaanite woman came crying to Jesus because her daughter was grievously oppressed by demons, Jesus rebuffed her. He told her that it was not wise to take the "children's bread" (believers) and give it to the dogs (non-believers). Please remember, this woman wanted Jesus to cast out the evil spirit that was oppressing her daughter. She was looking for deliverance. This passage proves that deliverance from demonic oppression is the children's bread (born-again believers).

This passage in the book of Matthew proves that deliverance from demonic oppression is a covenant right of God's children. The bread that Melchizedek gave to Abram was also the *bread of deliverance from demonic oppression*. It did not take long for Abram to discover how the bread of the Order of Melchizedek can deliver a person from demonic powers. When the king of Sodom arrived, he came on the scene accompanied by an avalanche of evil spirits from the underworld. But these demonic spirits could not touch or infect Abram with their poison because he had already partaken of the bread of deliverance. This is why I advise Kingdom businessmen and women to have Holy Communion with members of their staff, every week. They will get more business done this way and increase their company's profitability.

I really believe that New Testament churches that are either afraid of teaching on deliverance or do not believe in it are not patterning themselves after the Order of Melchizedek. The deliverance ministry is an integral part of the new creation Order of Melchizedek Priesthood. Jesus Christ, who is the High Priest of the Order of Melchizedek, cast more devils out of people than any other man in human history. How can we fully represent Jesus Christ if we do not believe in His deliverance ministry?

THE SACRED WINE

*And Melchizedek, the king of Salem and a priest of God Most High, brought Abram some bread and **wine** (emphasis added). Genesis 14:18*

The second vital spiritual element that Melchizedek gave to Abram when he intercepted him in the King's Valley was the "sacred wine." Understanding the prophetic symbolism of this sacred wine will usher us into a whole new dimension of life-giving revelation. Based upon the prophetic writings of the holy writ wine symbolizes the following:

1. **The Spirit of the Kingdom of God**

And do not get drunk with wine, for that is debauchery; but ever be filled and stimulated with the [Holy] Spirit. Speak out to one another in psalms and hymns and spiritual songs, offering praise with voices [and instruments] and making melody with all your heart to the Lord, At all times and for everything giving thanks in the name of our Lord Jesus Christ to God the Father. Ephesians 5:18-20 AMP

But if I am casting out demons by the Spirit of God, then the Kingdom of God has arrived among you. Matthew 12:28

We have already established the fact that the "Kingdom of God" is the primary ingredient of the true message of the Gospel and the only message that Jesus preached. But God's method for establishing His Kingdom here on earth is through the Person and work of the Holy Spirit. *The Holy Spirit is the spiritual Governor and Administrator of the Kingdom of God on earth.*

In the Garden of Eden Adam and Eve did not "lose a religion; they lost a Kingdom." So the most important ministerial assignment of the Holy Spirit is to restore the Kingdom of God to our troubled planet. The sacred wine that Melchizedek the King-Priest gave to Abram represents the indwelling presence of the Holy Spirit. The Holy Spirit is the Spirit of the Kingdom of God. *He is the One who drives the machinery of the Kingdom of God here on earth.* By giving Abram the sacred wine, Melchizedek wanted Abram to be saturated with the Spirit of the Kingdom (the Holy Spirit).

It is impossible to effectively advance the Kingdom of God on earth if we are not filled with the Spirit of Christ. We must be filled with the Holy Spirit to overflowing if we are serious about being "power brokers" in the Kingdom of God. I truly believe that churches and businessmen who are patterned after the Order of Melchizedek cannot help but be Kingdom driven and Kingdom minded. Unfortunately many pastors and Christians (born-again believers who are still trapped in the Christian religion) are more focused on building their personal empires than advancing the Kingdom of God.

2. Wine as an Intoxicating Agent

After the flood, Noah began to cultivate the ground, and he planted a vineyard. [21] One day he drank some wine he had made, and he became drunk and lay naked inside his tent. Genesis 9:20-21

Universally, wine is also known as an intoxicating agent. When people drink too much wine, it takes over the natural inclinations of their five physical senses. I remember living with an alcoholic uncle in the late '80s. He was probably one of the stingiest men I've ever met when he was sober. When he was sober, he would complain about the price of goods and services on anything that he saw. But the moment he got drunk, the alcohol had a very transforming effect on his personality.

Under the influence of alcohol my uncle became a very different person. He was happier and much more generous than usual. When I discovered this pattern about him, I stopped asking him for money when he was sober. Under the influence of strong wine my uncle also became much easier to talk to. The wine had intercepted his usual behavior patterns. The wine of the Holy Spirit also works in like manner; it intercepts our usual reactions to things. If we normally react in anger the wine of the Holy Spirit would have us react in a spirit of peace. This is why the wine of the Spirit is an important spiritual element in manifesting the technology of divine interception in the affairs of men.

> *The Holy Spirit is the spiritual Governor and Administrator of the Kingdom of God on earth.*

Correctional facilities (prisons) are full of men and women who are serving their sentence behind bars because they could not control their emotions in the heat of passion. In the heat of passion, some of them assaulted their friends and family. Under the Mountain of Law this is what is known as crimes of passion. There are people who are locked up for life, because they killed their spouse, friend, child, relative, employer, co-worker, teacher or pastor in the heat of passion. Not a day goes by when they do not wish they could take it all back. But it is already too late in the natural realm. The damage has already been done. This is why we need the supernatural wine and wisdom of the Holy Spirit to help intercept and heal the fragility of our own human emotions and our response to them, including triggers, hot buttons and flashbacks.

A CHANGED AND OBEDIENT HEART

But Samuel replied, "What is more pleasing to the LORD: your burnt offerings and sacrifices or your obedience to his voice? Listen! Obedience is better than sacrifice, and submission is better than offering the fat of rams. ²³ Rebellion is as sinful as witchcraft, and stubbornness as bad as worshiping idols. So because you have rejected the command of the LORD, he has rejected you as king."
1 Samuel 15:22-23

Him hath God exalted with his right hand to be a Prince and a Saviour, for to give repentance to Israel, and forgiveness of sins. ³²And we are his witnesses of these things; and so is also the Holy Ghost, whom God hath given to them that obey him. Acts 5:31-33 KJV

The fourth important element in the technology of divine interception is *a changed and obedient heart*. A changed and obedient heart is one of the key ingredients for manifesting this ancient spiritual technology in the affairs of men. If our heart has not been changed by the saving grace of our Lord Jesus Christ, the covenant of obedience to God will be very difficult for us to master. Obedience to God is not possible in the fallen Adamic nature. Christ must first change us internally before we can obey.

The unregenerate nature can never obey God. But after we are changed from the inside out, we can then respond more accurately to the technology of divine interception. In the absence of a changed and obedient heart there is nothing in us which can respond to the technology of divine interception. This is why King David cried to God to give him a clean heart, and renew a right spirit within him after he fell into sin with Bathsheba, the mother of King Solomon. When people have a changed and obedient heart, it's very easy for them to respond to the technology of divine interception whenever God initiates it.

TITHES OF HONOR

After Abram returned from his victory over Kedorlaomer and all his allies, the king of Sodom went out to meet him in the valley of Shaveh (that is, the King's Valley). [18] And Melchizedek, the king of Salem and a priest of God Most High, brought Abram some bread and wine. [19] Melchizedek blessed Abram with this blessing: "Blessed be Abram by God Most High, Creator of heaven and earth. [20] And blessed be God Most High, who has defeated your enemies for you." Then Abram gave Melchizedek a tenth of all the goods he had recovered. [21] The king of Sodom said to Abram, "Give back my people who were captured. But you may keep for yourself all the goods you have recovered." [22] Abram replied to the king of Sodom, "I solemnly swear to the LORD, God Most High, Creator of heaven and earth, [23] that I will not take so much as a single thread or sandal thong from what belongs to you. Otherwise you might say, 'I am the one who made Abram rich.' [24]I will accept only what my young warriors have already eaten, and I request that you give a fair share of the goods to my allies—

Aner, Eshcol, and Mamre." Genesis 14:17-24

One of the defining moments in the encounter that Abram had with Melchizedek had to do with the covenant exchange that took place between Melchizedek and Abram. The Bible tells us that Melchizedek, who was representing the Godhead in this supernatural transaction, gave Abram sacred bread and wine. Abram, on the other hand, who was representing "humanity" in this heavenly transaction, responded by sowing "tithes of honor" into this divine priesthood.

> *A changed and obedient heart is one of the key ingredients for manifesting this ancient spiritual technology in the affairs of men.*

Please remember that in this divine transaction Melchizedek was sent to intercept Abram before the king of Sodom got to him. This interception was Melchizedek's primary assignment besides bringing Abram into a living covenant with God. When Melchizedek showed up in the King's Valley, he brought with him a spiritual atmosphere full of divine interception.

Since Abram was inspired by God to respond to Melchizedek's interception by giving tithes of all it follows then the best way for Kingdom citizens to manifest the technology of divine interception is to participate in the giving of tithes to God. Since the whole concept of tithing was birthed in an atmosphere saturated with divine interception, it is safe to say that tithing excites the manifestation of the technology of divine interception. This is why tithing is the fifth most important element, which encompasses the mechanics of manifesting the technology of divine interception on the human plane. For more on this important topic, please refer to my book *The Lost Key: Tithing Under the Order of Melchizedek*. Suffice it to say for now that tithing under the Order of Melchizedek is superior to and different than tithing under the Order of Levi, since Jesus (and Melchizedek as a foreshadowing of him) is both a King & Priest, whereas the Levitical priesthood is entirely devoid of the kingly nature and authority.

THE MECHANICS OF THE TECHNOLOGY OF DIVINE INTERCEPTION

LIFE APPLICATION SECTION

MEMORY VERSE

To every thing there is a season, and a time to every purpose under the heaven: Ecclesiastes 3:1 KJV

REFLECTIONS

Write down the Key ingredients that make up the Mechanics of the Technology of Divine Interception.

_____

_____

_____

_____

_____

_____

What role does "Kairos" play in manifesting the Technology of Divine Interception?

_____

_____

_____

_____

_____

_____

JOURNAL YOUR THOUGHTS

_____

_____

_____

_____

_____

_____

_____

_____

_____

_____

_____

_____

_____

_____

_____

_____

_____

_____

_____

_____

_____

_____

_____

_____

_____

_____

_____

_____

_____

_____

_____

THE MECHANICS OF THE TECHNOLOGY OF DIVINE INTERCEPTION

CHAPTER ELEVEN
THE VEHICLES OF DIVINE INTERCEPTION

In this chapter we will examine the vehicles that God has established to help manifest the technology of divine interception here on earth. These vehicles are channels or portals that God uses to initiate this ancient spiritual technology in the lives of those He has chosen to intercept. If we refuse to recognize these portals as vehicles of divine interception, then we will miss our moment(s) of divine visitation. We will miss our moment(s) of rescue.

By definition a "Vehicle" is any means in or by which someone travels or something is carried or conveyed; it is a means of transport. This chapter will examine the different vehicles that God uses to manifest the technology of divine interception on the human plane.

THE GODHEAD

For there are three that bear record in heaven, the Father, the Word, and the Holy Ghost: and these three are one. 1 John 5:7

THE VEHICLES OF DIVINE INTERCEPTION

The greatest mystery in all of creation concerns the Trinity. This is a divine mystery that is beyond the comprehension of mind and science. This divine eternal mystery can only be understood by faith and revelation. The Scriptures tell us that there is one God (James 2:19) who expresses His deity in three distinct persons, in the same way that man is "one" and yet he is "spirit, soul and body." Paul the Apostle called this triune nature of the one God, the "Godhead," which consists of God the Father, God the Son and God the Holy Spirit.

Since the technology of divine interception is always initiated by God, the triune members of the Godhead are intricately involved in how this technology is transported to the event, subject or persons being intercepted. Said simply the Godhead is the first and most important vehicle of the technology of divine interception, and this fact alone explains why it is so powerful. Demonic powers have zero chance of overturning the bus if God is the one driving it. "If God is for us, who can be against us?" (Rom. 8:31).

We will now examine three Scripture passages where the members of the Godhead volunteered their services and became vehicles of divine interception.

> *Then they said, "Come, let's build a great city for ourselves with a tower that reaches into the sky. This will make us famous and keep us from being scattered all over the world." ⁵ But the LORD came down to look at the city and the tower the people were building. ⁶ "Look!" he said. "The people are united, and they all speak the same language. After this, nothing they set out to do will be impossible for them! ⁷ Come, let's go down and confuse the people with different languages. Then they won't be able to understand each other." Genesis 11:4-7*

The Great Commission that Jesus Christ gave to the Church at the end of His Messianic ministry was nothing new. He was simply reinstating God's original plan to plant the Kingdom of God here on earth. In Genesis 11:4-7 the human race rallied around a demonic agenda to build a tower toward heaven instead of spreading the influence of God's invisible Kingdom here on earth. It would seem that all the inhabitants of the earth at the time were well aware that God wanted to scatter them across the seven continents to expand the rule of the Kingdom of heaven over the planet Earth. But instead of obeying the divine Kingdom mandate the inhabitants of the earth under the leadership of a demonized leader named "Nimrod" decided to build a religious tower toward heaven.

> *The Godhead is the first and most important vehicle of the technology of divine interception.*

It is worth noting that what happened at the tower of Babel gives us the marked difference between the Kingdom and religion. All world religions from antiquity have been obsessed with the idea of "going to heaven or going up" whereas the Kingdom is obsessed with the idea of God's government "coming down" to the earth. In this case God the Father was the vehicle of interception that moved on the other members of the Godhead to collectively intercept a diabolical religious spirit, which was seducing all of humanity to abandon the global expansion of the Kingdom here on earth.

"Simon, Simon, Satan has asked to sift each of you like wheat. [32] But I have pleaded in prayer for you, Simon, that your faith should not fail. So when you have repented and turned to me again, strengthen your brothers." Luke 22:31

In Luke 22:31 we have a very revealing incident that shows Christ (God the Word) volunteering Himself as the vehicle of interception against a demonically engineered plot to destroy Peter the Apostle. The devil and his demonic cohorts had set their sight on annihilating Peter's faith in God using his own inherent character flaws, but Jesus Christ intercepted the demonic transmissions about Peter.

After Christ intercepted the demonic transmissions against Peter, He began to pray ferociously against the demonic agenda gaining ground or bearing fruit in Peter's life. By the time Jesus Christ made Peter aware of the demonic conspiracy against him, the demonic technology against Peter had lost most of its poison. Christ's prayers had neutralized and redirected the impact of the demonic agenda against Peter into something positive. The devil had planned to take Peter through an "irreparable" faith crush. But Christ's prayer placed a "divine restraining order" on the demonic conspiracy, so that instead of Peter going through a "faith crush" his fall from grace ended up strengthening Peter and converting him into a "bond servant" of Jesus Christ.

> *Next Paul and Silas traveled through the area of Phrygia and Galatia, because the Holy Spirit had prevented them from preaching the word in the province of Asia at that time. [7] Then coming to the borders of Mysia, they headed north for the province of Bithynia, but again the Spirit of Jesus did not allow them to go there. [8] So instead, they went on through Mysia to the seaport of Troas. [9] That night Paul had a vision: A man from Macedonia in northern Greece was standing there, pleading with him, "Come over to Macedonia and help us!" [10] So we decided to leave for Macedonia at once, having concluded that God was calling us to preach the Good News there. Acts 16:6-10*

In Acts 16:6-10 we see the involvement of the third member of the Godhead in the technology of divine interception. In this case the Holy Spirit is the one being used as the vehicle of divine interception. Paul the Apostle and his apprentice Silas were traveling through parts of Asia and they wanted to preach the gospel there, but the Holy Spirit intercepted their course of action and stopped them from preaching in this Asian province. Then they tried to preach the gospel in Bithynia, a city in present day Greece, but the Holy Spirit intercepted their decision again.

The above passage of Scripture barks against those who feel like God wants us to preach the gospel to everybody at any given time. While Paul and Silas were sleeping, the Holy Spirit gave Paul a prophetic dream which unmasked the "purpose of the divine interception." The reason the Holy Spirit stopped Paul and Silas from preaching the gospel in Bithynia was because they were in a time of "Kairos" (a divine appointed time) that God had established in the spirit world to intercept the Philippian jailer in the city of Macedonia. This Philippian prison warden ended up becoming the senior pastor of the church in Philippi. Had Paul and Silas not responded to the divine interception which stopped them from going into Bythinia, they would have lost precious time in the realm of the spirit. They would have missed the "Kairos" of God for the Philippian Jailer. By definition "Kairos" is a supernatural window in time where all forces divine and natural converge into a specific pocket of time to accelerate the fulfillment of God's purpose. These special pockets of time are very difficult to replace or manufacture in time. Sometimes it takes years for us to spiritually and financially recover from having missed one moment of "Kairos."

ANGELS

After the wise men were gone, an angel of the Lord appeared to Joseph in a dream. "Get up! Flee to Egypt with the child and his mother," the angel said. "Stay there until I tell you to return, because Herod is going to search for the child to kill him." [14] That night Joseph left for Egypt with the child and Mary, his mother. Matthew 2:13-14

Angels are some of the most glorious beings in all of God's creation. They were and are the original sons of God. They were created by God before He created mankind. They have a spiritual or celestial body which can never die in the same way that our physical bodies die. They have an inbuilt technology of transport that enables them to travel at the speed of light and thought. Since they derive their energy from living in the presence of God they never get tired and they excel in strength (Ps. 103). These holy angels are extremely zealous for the Kingdom and are completely loyal to God and His will.

Like mankind the angels were created perfect and innocent, but not holy. The condition of Holiness can only exist in a person/creature that has been tempted but chose to rise above the temptation in order to please God. When Lucifer gave in to sin and led one third of the angels of God into a colossal insurrection against God's government, the remaining two thirds who refused to join the rebellion instantly became "holy angels." The inherent nature of these angels went from "innocence" to "holiness," while the nature of the angels who followed Lucifer became set in evil. This would explain why God uses His holy angels in many instances as vehicles of divine interception. They are so holy that they will never succumb to the sin nature of those that God has assigned them to intercept.

In Matthew 2:13-14 the angel Gabriel appeared to Joseph in his dream and told him to take the baby Jesus and his wife Mary to Egypt for a period of two years. The angel informed him that King Herod was planning to assassinate the newborn child. In this case the angel who appeared to Joseph in the divinely engineered prophetic dream was the vehicle of interception that God used to initiate the technology of divine interception in order to preempt the demonic agenda to kill the Son of God before His time. Angels are intricately connected to the technology of divine interception. A couple of times angels have intercepted demonic technologies that would have destroyed me.

Very early the next morning, the king got up and hurried out to the lions' den. [20] *When he got there, he called out in anguish, "Daniel, servant of the living God! Was your God, whom you serve so faithfully, able to rescue you from the lions?"* [21] *Daniel answered, "Long live the king!* [22] *My God sent his angel to shut the lions' mouths so that they would not hurt me, for I have been found innocent in his sight. And I have not wronged you, Your Majesty."* [23] *The king was overjoyed and ordered that Daniel be lifted from the den. Not a scratch was found on him, for he had trusted in his God. Daniel 6:19-23*

> **Angels are intricately connected to the technology of divine interception.**

One of the greatest incidents of divine interception in the Old Testament concerns the supernatural deliverance of the prophet Daniel from the lion's den. Daniel had risen to a place of favor and prominence in the Persian Empire led by King Darius. King Darius loved and favored Daniel so much that he set him as the supreme prime minister over the whole kingdom. Daniel's position of favor in the Persian Empire struck a cord of jealousy in some prominent Persian politicians, who engineered a diabolical plot to destroy Daniel's life, influence and reputation with the king.

These jealous politicians came into a demonic political alliance and deceived King Darius into making a very presumptuous decree. They manipulated the king into making a decree that anyone who worshipped and prayed to any God other than King Darius was going to be thrown into the lion's den. These envious and demonically-inspired politicians knew that Daniel would never bow or pray to any God other than the God of Abraham, Isaac and Jacob. True to their assessment, Daniel refused to obey the king's decree, and he was arrested and thrown into the lion's den.

His political foes were certain that they had secured Daniel's death and eliminated his growing influence with King Darius. But they were dead wrong. In their devious plot they had not factored in the role that the technology of divine interception would play in Daniel's deliverance. They did not know that Daniel belonged to the "Unshakable Kingdom," which is serviced by this powerful ancient spiritual technology that has delivered countless Kingdom citizens through the ages. Kingdom citizens who work in the corridors of Government need to learn to cooperate with the technology of divine interception to escape devious political schemes against them.

While Daniel's enemies were rejoicing and toasting to his misfortune, God sent a company of warring angels into the lion's den before Daniel was thrown in as the sun was setting. These angels shut the mouths of the lions and perhaps even suppressed the normal appetite for human flesh in these otherwise ravenous predators. These "king of the jungle" lions were sleeping in Daniel's lap like house puppies. Early the next morning following Daniel's imprisonment in the lion's den, King Darius, who had spent a sleepless night interceding for Daniel, ran to the lion's den hoping against hope that his dear friend Daniel had survived the ordeal. The desperate king called for Daniel to come out of the lion's den if he was still alive.

Daniel answered the king that the Living God had sent his holy angels as vehicles of divine interception to protect him because there was no wickedness found in Daniel against either his God or the king. When Daniel's political foes heard of Daniel's amazing deliverance from the lion's den, they were overcome with fear. They realized that their diabolical plot had failed miserably. They could hear the engines of death churning in their direction. They knew the king had discovered that they had deceived and manipulated him into signing this death decree and participating in their evil plot. King Darius commanded his officials to throw them and their families into the same lion's den that they had put Daniel in. The lions in the den did not even take the time to say grace over the food that they were about to receive. They overpowered and devoured Daniel's enemies in short order, in a matter of seconds and minutes, respectively, like a thirsty man devours water in a scorched desert.

PROPHETIC MESSENGERS

When the king of Aram was at war with Israel, he would confer with his officers and say, "We will mobilize our forces at such and such a place." ⁹ But immediately Elisha, the man of God, would warn the king of Israel, "Do not go near that place, for the Arameans are planning to mobilize their troops there." ¹⁰ So the king of Israel would send word to the place indicated by the man of God. Time and again Elisha warned the king, so that he would be on the alert there. ¹¹ The king of Aram became very upset over this. He called his officers together and demanded, "Which of you is the traitor? Who has been informing the king of Israel of my plans?" ¹² "It's not us, my lord the king," one of the officers replied. "Elisha, the prophet in Israel, tells the king of Israel even the words you speak in the privacy of your bedroom!" 2 Kings 6:8-12

In 2 Kings 6:8-12 we have a very interesting account that denotes how the technology of divine interception can assist world leaders in securing the affairs of the state. The above passage of Scripture also underscores why God wants His Church to rediscover the technology of divine interception. God want His Church, especially His apostolic leaders, to become skilled at operating in this technology so that they can help intercept diabolical demonic agendas against their countries of residence. Operating in the technology of divine interception on a national level will give the Church a platform of immense credibility before world leaders. In most nations the Church is despised and lightly esteemed because the world sees the Church as a religious institution that can speak to issues of the after-life but is impotent or incompetent in its ability to address current affairs of the state. The world's perception of the Church will change rapidly when both the Church and its marketplace leaders begin to operate skillfully in the technology of divine interception.

In 2 Kings 6:8-12, the Lord was using the prophet Elisha, as the primary vehicle of the technology of divine interception over the nation of Israel. On several occasions the prophet of God was able to intercept the military plots of the king of Syria against the nation of Israel. Elisha was such a skilled player in manifesting the technology of divine interception that he completely frustrated the efforts of the king of Syria. The king of Syria held a special meeting with his military counsel convinced that there was a "mole" in his camp who was selling their military intelligence to the king of Israel. One of his special advisors told him that there was no "mole" among his top military staff, but Elisha the Prophet was the one responsible for frustrating and intercepting their closely guarded intelligence.

> *The world's perception of the Church will change rapidly when both the Church and its marketplace leaders begin to operate skillfully in the technology of divine interception.*

The king of Syria quickly reorganized his military strategy around capturing the prophet Elisha in order to stop him from being the vehicle of the technology of divine interception. His vast armies of highly skilled warriors and mercenaries surrounded the prophet's residence, showcasing just how much the devil fears men and women of God who are skilled at operating in the technology of divine interception. Let me ask you a question: *"What kind of credibility do you think the prophet Elisha had with the king of Israel?"* The answer is obvious. He had great credibility with the king of Israel and his royal government. Let me ask you another important question: *"What kind of credibility do you think Church and marketplace leaders will have with their nation's government, when they begin assisting their government to intercept serious security threats against the homeland?"* I believe that the Church's credibility before the world will shoot through the roof.

Indeed, the Sovereign LORD never does anything, until he reveals his plans to his servants the prophets. Amos 3:7

The point I am trying to drive home is simply this; one of God's favorite vehicles for manifesting the technology of divine interception here on earth is His "prophets or prophetic messengers." From antiquity to the present day, God still uses prophetic messengers to manifest this ancient spiritual technology here on earth. This is why I love prophets and prophetic people. God has used them several times to save me from near disasters. This is why Kingdom citizens who do not believe in "prophets or the prophetic" are going to have a hard time cooperating with the technology of divine interception. They will rush through divine "Stop Signs or Red Lights" like an untamed wild horse or a bull in a china shop. The many disasters in commerce that transpire each year in the lives of many Kingdom citizens and entrepreneurs underscore the importance of manifesting the technology of divine interception in the marketplace.

Churches or spiritual leaders who do not embrace or believe in prophets or the prophetic will have a very difficult time operating in the technology of divine interception. This is because every spiritual technology or institution within the economy of the Kingdom is driven by a prophetic process. This is why not even Jesus Christ could come into the world without being preceded by a prophet like John the Baptist. John the Baptist was the physical embodiment of the prophetic technology and process that God used to introduce Jesus as the Messiah to the rest of the world. The prophetic process is to spiritual technology what gas is to the engine of a car. This is why God loves to use men and women who are anointed and skilled at manifesting prophetic technology on the human plane as vehicles of divine interception.

THE WORD OF GOD

How can a young person stay pure? By obeying your word. [10]
I have tried hard to find you— don't let me wander from your

commands. [11] I have hidden your word in my heart, that I might not sin against you. Psalm 119:9-11

For the word of God is alive and powerful. It is sharper than the sharpest two-edged sword, cutting between soul and spirit, between joint and marrow. It exposes our innermost thoughts and desires. Hebrews 4:12

The chronicles of both biblical and secular history testify to the "staying power" of what followers of Christ affectionately call the Bible. This ageless book that many people of faith claim to be the infallible Word of God, has been the subject and object of some of the meanest demonically engineered slander aimed at annihilating this holy book's influence on society. After nearly a hundred years of communism the Soviet Union splintered into several warring political factions, while the presence of the Bible that the communist regime had tried so hard to destroy has increased exponentially. In resisting the spread of the Word of God (Bible) in the Soviet Union, the communist regime only succeeded at destroying itself. This is why the eternal, infallible Word of God is one of the best vehicles available for the technology of divine interception.

> *Every spiritual technology or institution with the economy of the Kingdom is driven by a prophetic process.*

I have personally lost count of the number of times that God's word came into my heart and intercepted a demonic philosophy or lifestyle in my life. The apostle Paul tells us that the Word of God is sharper than any two-edged sword because it is the only one that can divide what is truly "spiritual" from what is "soulish and fleshly." For most people of faith the inability to divide the spirit from the soul has caused many to miss moments of divine interception until it was too late to change course.

A couple of years back my marriage was on the rocks. My wife and I were constantly arguing about things. At the time we both despised being married to each other, even though we loved each other deeply. The atmosphere of ongoing strife in our home was palpable. While we were going through this season of stress, I was invited to speak for a church in Chicago. This church placed me in a very luxurious hotel the day before the scheduled service. I felt very guilty basking in this luxurious suite knowing that trouble was brewing over my home. In desperation I cried to the Lord. "Lord, what is wrong with my marriage?" The answer came immediately but it was sharper than a double-edged sword. "You are fighting to be right instead of striving to be scriptural. I never called you to be right; I called you to be scriptural," God responded.

This Word from the Lord struck at the core of the strife and confusion that was driving my marriage to the edges of annihilation. I had been intercepted by the Word of God. This became the turning point of my life and marriage. In my case the Word of God, which I love dearly, was the vehicle God used to manifest the technology of divine interception. This is why Kingdom citizens, who do not have a driving passion to read and study the Word of God, will miss many great moments of divine interception.

PROPHETIC VISIONS AND DREAMS

When it was time to leave, they returned to their own country by another route, for God had warned them in a dream not to return to Herod. [13] After the wise men were gone, an angel of the Lord appeared to Joseph in a dream. "Get up! Flee to Egypt with the child and his mother," the angel said. "Stay there until I tell you to return, because Herod is going to search for the child to kill him." [14] That night Joseph left for Egypt with the child and Mary, his mother, Matthew 2:12-14

At this juncture we will look at two more vehicles that God uses frequently to manifest the technology of divine interception on the human plane. These two vehicles are "prophetic visions and dreams." The primary difference between these two vehicles is rooted in how they manifest on the human plane. Prophetic visions usually manifest when the recipient or the person being intercepted is wide awake, whereas prophetic dreams usually manifest when the recipient or person being intercepted is asleep.

In Matthew 2:12-14 an angel of God (I believe it was the angel Gabriel) appeared to Joseph in a dream and warned him of the demonic conspiracy to kill the baby Jesus by King Herod. The angel of God told him to take the baby Jesus and his wife to the country of Egypt where he resided for two years. Had Joseph failed to heed the divine interception that came in his dream, he would have jeopardized Christ's messianic mission to the world. Fortunately Joseph heeded the prophetic warning of the angel and saved his family from the impending demonic attack that was brewing through King Herod. Had Joseph been disobedient to what the angel had told him in his dream, he would have nullified the technology of the divine interception.

Joseph responded, "Both of Pharaoh's dreams mean the same thing. God is telling Pharaoh in advance what he is about to do. ²⁶ The seven healthy cows and the seven healthy heads of grain both represent seven years of prosperity. ²⁷ The seven thin, scrawny cows that came up later and the seven thin heads of grain, withered by the east wind, represent seven years of famine. ²⁸ "This will happen just as I have described it, for God has revealed to Pharaoh in advance what he is about to do. ²⁹ The next seven years will be a period of great prosperity throughout the land of Egypt. ³⁰ But afterward there will be seven years of famine so great that all the prosperity will be forgotten in Egypt. Famine will destroy the land. ³¹ This famine will be so severe that even the memory of the good years will be erased. ³² As for having two similar dreams, it means that these events have been decreed by God, and he will soon make them happen. Genesis 41:25-32

The rise of the young Hebrew boy Joseph to a position of prominence in a foreign land where he was sold into slavery has marveled the minds of seekers and dreamers for centuries. From the cradle of his humble beginnings in the land of Palestine, this young and handsome Hebrew boy manifested an unusual gift of interpreting dreams. Coincidentally it was Joseph's uncanny ability to communicate with God through the "dream dimension" that landed him in serious trouble with his own brothers.

His brothers resented him because he had stolen their father's affection and also for his dreams which predicted that they would be in servitude to him in the future destiny. Little did his envious brothers know that the dreams they hated him for would later become the basis for the divine interception that would save them and the entire world. Joseph's brothers did not know that dreams are among the vehicles that God uses to manifest the technology of divine interception on the human plane.

It is this same uncanny ability to interpret and communicate with God through dreams that ushered him into a position of immense political prominence after he interpreted Pharaoh's dream. In what would otherwise have been a typical day in prison, Joseph was snatched out of the prison house in royal grandeur. The chariots of the Egyptian king had been summoned to pick him up and escort him to the royal palace.

Joseph was ushered through the royal courts to the throne room where Pharaoh was seated in great distress surrounded by his anxious cabinet and his team of perplexed magicians who had failed to interpret the dream which was at the center of Pharaoh's distress. Pharaoh was convinced his dreams were of critical importance to the future of Egypt but none of his magicians had a clue as to the true meaning of his dreams.

When the young Hebrew prophet was ushered before the king of Egypt, Pharaoh rehearsed his dreams to Joseph. When he was finished recounting his dreams to Joseph, Joseph's uncanny ability for interpreting dreams kicked into high gear. The interpretation that the former Hebrew slave gave to Pharaoh left him breathless and speechless. Joseph made it very clear to Pharaoh that the dreams that God had given him were meant to intercept and minimize the impact of a very serious global famine which was rapidly approaching. Joseph also gave Pharaoh uncanny business advice on how to store enough grain throughout the land of Egypt which would preserve Egypt in the days of the famine. Pharaoh was so impressed with Joseph's uncanny business acumen that he made him lord of Egypt. Fueled by the future prophetic implications of Pharaoh's dreams, Joseph became a zealot at the task of storing as much grain as he could during the seven years of plenty. Joseph's ability to recognize that Pharaoh's dreams were simply vehicles of the technology of divine interception saved an entire generation of nations from complete annihilation through the worst economic recession in recorded human history. This is why citizens of the Kingdom of God must never treat prophetic dreams lightly. All God ordained prophetic dreams come embedded with either the spirit of interception or prophetic keys that can unlock your future destiny.

> *The next day as Cornelius's messengers were nearing the town, Peter went up on the flat roof to pray. It was about noon, [10] and he was hungry. But while a meal was being prepared, he fell into a trance. [11] He saw the sky open, and something like a large sheet was let down by its four corners. [12] In the sheet were all sorts of animals, reptiles, and birds. [13] Then a voice said to him, "Get up, Peter; kill and eat them." Acts 10:9-13*

The above passage of Scripture meanders into the second vehicle that God uses frequently to manifest the technology of divine interception. This vehicle is called "visions." This vehicle of interception (visions) comes in three main forms, namely:

1. Trance Visions

2. Open Visions

3. Mental impressions

The prophetic vision that Peter the Apostle had in Acts chapter ten is what the Bible calls a "trance." A trance is a prophetic vision in which the person experiencing this type of vision is in a semi-conscious state. In most cases the person having such a vision does not know whether they were in the body or out of it, but the aftereffects of the vision are very real.

In Peter's case the Lord placed him in a trance in order to intercept his Judaic orthodox thinking which was standing in the way of God's desire to introduce the gospel of the Kingdom to the Gentiles or non-Jews. As an orthodox religious Jew, Peter's upbringing made it difficult for him to be an unbiased preacher and teacher to the Gentiles. In his orthodox Jewish mind, mixing with Gentiles was a practice in ceremonial uncleanness. What Peter did not know is that his orthodox mentality was keeping him from being a key player in the greater unfolding plan of God to reach nations with the gospel of the Kingdom.

On April 23, as I was standing on the bank of the great Tigris River, [5] I looked up and saw a man dressed in linen clothing, with a belt of pure gold around his waist. [6] His body looked like a precious gem. His face flashed like lightning, and his eyes flamed like torches. His arms and feet shone like polished bronze, and his voice roared like a vast multitude of people. [7] Only I, Daniel, saw this vision. The men with me saw nothing, but they were suddenly terrified and ran away to hide. [8] So I was left there all alone to see this amazing vision. My strength left me, my face grew deathly pale, and I felt very weak. [9] Then I heard the man speak, and when I heard the sound of his voice, I fainted and lay there with my face to the ground. Daniel 10:4-9

On the other hand the prophetic vision that Daniel had is what is known as an "open vision." In an open vision the person experiencing the vision is wide awake. This means that in an open vision the person experiencing the vision retains the full use of their physical senses. In Daniel's case he was aware of where he was (location) and the geography of the location when the vision happened. Daniel was also aware of the men who were with him when God gave him an open vision.

In Daniel's case, the open vision was the vehicle that God was using to intercept future events and Daniel's ability to understand the future destiny of God's people in the last days. This particular open vision in Daniel's life has helped millions of seekers through the ages navigate and interpret current events in the light of what God showed Daniel would happen in the last days. I really believe that many Kingdom citizens and marketplace leaders are going to be intercepted by God using open visions as vehicles of divine interception.

FERVENT PRAYER

"Simon, Simon, Satan has asked to sift each of you like wheat. [32] But I have pleaded in prayer for you, Simon, that your faith should not fail. So when you have repented and turned to me again, strengthen your brothers." Luke 22:31-32

Legendary author E.M. Bounds says that he who is weak in prayer is weak as a factor in God's work, for the work of God is powered by the fuel of fervent prayer. Dr. Myles Munroe in his bestselling book, *The Power and Purpose of Prayer,* defines prayer as earthly license for heavenly interference. In my humble opinion the power of "fervent prayer" is rooted in the fact that God responds to the fervent prayer of the righteous. This would then explain why prayer is one of God's favorite vehicles for manifesting the technology of divine interception.

Perhaps one of the most impactful events involving fervent prayer as a vehicle of the technology of divine interception involves the prayer of protection and interception that Jesus prayed over Peter. According to Luke 22:31, Jesus had supernaturally intercepted a diabolical conspiracy of the enemy that was designed to destroy Peter's faith and destiny. Jesus told Peter that He had prayed for him and preempted the devil's primary objective. What was left of the devil's initial plan was transformed into a spiritual apostolic development course to strengthen Peter for his future destiny. This is why spiritual atmospheres that are saturated with fervent prayer are full of the spirit of divine interception.

When Herod saw how much this pleased the Jewish people, he also arrested Peter. (This took place during the Passover celebration.) ⁴ Then he imprisoned him, placing him under the guard of four squads of four soldiers each. Herod intended to bring Peter out for public trial after the Passover. ⁵ But while Peter was in prison, the church prayed very earnestly for him. ⁶ The night before Peter was to be placed on trial, he was asleep, fastened with two chains between two soldiers. Others stood guard at the prison gate. ⁷ Suddenly, there was a bright light in the cell, and an angel of the Lord stood before Peter. The angel struck him on the side to awaken him and said, "Quick! Get up!" And the chains fell off his wrists. Acts 12:3-7

Legendary author E.M. Bounds says that he who is weak in prayer is weak as a factor in God's work, for the work of God is powered by the fuel of fervent prayer.

Interestingly enough Peter the Apostle became the recipient of another prayer-engineered divine interception, when he was imprisoned by King Herod. King Herod saw that he could raise his political clout with the Sanhedrin council by persecuting the Church, especially the apostles. He killed James the brother of John and then he imprisoned Peter, intending to kill him after the Passover.

But the Church community got together and offered corporate fervent prayer before God for Peter's deliverance. Their fervent prayers became the vehicle of the technology of divine interception. While Peter was bound in chains in the innermost part of the prison an angel of God showed up. At the majestic presence of the angel of God all of Peter's chains fell off and all the prison doors opened of their own accord. This amazing interception would have seemed far fetched had it not been supported by the Bible. But this amazing interception serves as a reminder to all Kingdom citizens and entrepreneurs that the technology of divine interception is very common in spiritual climates that are birthed in prayer. Millions of dollars in Kingdom resources are lost each year to the enemy because many vehicles of commerce that are led by Kingdom marketplace leaders are not powered by the spirit of ongoing prayer. I really believe that if many Kingdom entrepreneurs would simply take fervent prayer seriously there would be many instances of mind boggling divine interceptions.

A MULTITUDE OF COUNSELORS

Plans go wrong for lack of advice; many advisers bring success. Proverbs 15:22

King Solomon is the wisest and richest person who has ever lived. If God allowed you to travel through time for a special meeting to consult with King Solomon, how would you prepare yourself for such a once in a lifetime opportunity? How much would you be willing to pay to secure an audience with such a famous and wealthy king? Would you argue with King Solomon if he gave you advice on life, government or business, or would you embrace his counsel like your life depended on it? Unless you were mentally challenged I really believe that you would do the latter.

Only the foolish and rebellious ones would stand in the presence of a king of King Solomon's stature and argue with the wisdom of a sage. If God ever gave me such an opportunity I would take my pen and notepad and write down every word of wisdom that would permeate his mouth. Even though this wise king is dead, his writings are still speaking to us today. King Solomon's wise sayings are just as relevant today as they were when he first penned them. This is because King Solomon's words were inspired by God Almighty.

In his famous proverbs (Prov. 15:22) King Solomon made a very startling observation. He tells us that most plans go wrong for the lack of advice. But King Solomon also noted that consulting many advisers or experts within their field brought great success to the business or war plans of those who were diligent enough to seek such wise counsel. Proverbs 15:22 unmasks one of the most powerful vehicles of the technology of divine interception that God uses quite often. This vehicle is called "Multitude of Counselors." Several times in my life God has intercepted diabolical assignments of the enemy against me because of the wise counsel of my Multitude of Counselors. Yet I have also seen young ministers or entrepreneurs who are paying a heavy price for refusing to heed the wise counsel of a Multitude of Counselors that God had set in their path. Whenever we frustrate the technology of divine interception we will also suffer the consequences of our actions.

Perhaps the best example which illustrates the importance of heeding the technology of divine interception through the vehicle of a Multitude of Counselors is found in 1 Kings 12.

Then King Rehoboam discussed the matter with the older men who had counseled his father, Solomon. "What is your advice?" he asked. "How should I answer these people?" ⁷ The older counselors replied, "If you are willing to be a servant to these people today and give them a favorable answer, they will always be your loyal subjects." ⁸ But Rehoboam rejected the advice of the older men and instead asked the opinion of the young men who had grown up with him and were now his advisers. 1 Kings 12:6-8

Ironically the canvas for this regrettable story is the short lived reign of Rehoboam, Solomon's successor. Even though his father was the wisest and richest man who has ever lived, this young king was a fool. Rehoboam's horrific reign over the nation of Israel proves that divine wisdom is not genetic; it is an endowment of God.

After his coronation as king, young Rehoboam made a great decision which he later reversed to his own detriment. He gathered a "Multitude of wise counselors" and asked for their opinion as to how he should rule. The counsel of wise men gave the young king great advice that would have endeared him to his citizens had he followed through. But to their dismay he scorned their wise counsel in favor of the "untested counsel" of his young peers. His young peers told the young king to treat his subjects more harshly than any previous king before him. No advice would have been any more fatal than what the young king was given by his coalition of inexperienced advisers. The people of Israel revolted against the young king's authority and ten of the twelve tribes of Israel left the young king's dominion and formed their own kingdom. What an unnecessary tragedy. But it is further proof that no one can ignore the technology of divine interception and get away with it. There is always a heavy price tag involving pain and suffering that is attached to ignoring vehicles and technologies of divine interception.

MEMORY

"A few days later this younger son packed all his belongings and moved to a distant land, and there he wasted all his money in wild living. [14] About the time his money ran out, a great famine swept over the land, and he began to starve. [15] He persuaded a local farmer to hire him, and the man sent him into his fields to feed the pigs. [16] The young man became so hungry that even the pods he was feeding the pigs looked good to him. But no one gave him anything. [17] "When he finally came to his senses, he said to himself, 'At home even the hired servants have food enough to spare, and here I am dying of hunger! [18] I will go home to my father and say, "Father, I have sinned against both heaven and you, [19] and I am no longer worthy of being called your son.

Please take me on as a hired servant."' [20] *"So he returned home to his father. And while he was still a long way off, his father saw him coming. Filled with love and compassion, he ran to his son, embraced him, and kissed him. Luke 15:13-20*

"Among all of God's creation, the human body, especially the brain, is the most intricate, complex and marvelous design, allowing 'mind-body communications' to be constantly adapting to a changing environment and personal experiences. One such marvel is the function of memory, storage, retrieval and man's ability to develop an internal model of the 'reality' of the external world. By using such a 'model' or internal representation, we interpret sensory inputs and device 'meaning' out of what's happening to us and around us.

We are constantly 'evaluating' multitudes of incoming information, 'comparing' with what is 'already stored in the memories.' Depending on the nature of such evaluation and interpretation (along with the chemical contents in the body), we may experience great joy and exuberance, confidence, motivation, etc, or we may experience fear, anger, sorrow, suspicion, etc. Memories influence every action, pattern of reaction and choices we make. Memories can sabotage our chances for success and effectiveness, or memories can serve us great rewards."

(Overcomers Teachers Manual, by Dr. Aiko Hormann, Brain Scientist)

Nothing baffles scientists more than the genius engineering of the human brain. The human brain is the best supercomputer in the world today. Many of the intricate functions of the brain are yet to be discovered, but what has already been discovered has caused many scientists to baffle in awe. Any arguments for evolution dissipate when the brain becomes the object of discussion because its complexity lends itself to the idea of intelligent design.

Among the many functions of the brain few have captured the imagination of scientists and inspired more studies than the brain's capacity for memory and memory storage. The brain through its function of memory can store vast amounts of data, analyze that data and create a response profile based upon data stored in the memory. This is one of the reasons why God uses the brain's function of memory as one of the vehicles of the technology of divine interception. God used the memory of the prodigal son about his father's house to "intercept" and deliver him from living an illicit lifestyle in a foreign country.

There is not enough space in this writing for me to tell you about the number of times that God has intercepted me from making a mistake using the vehicle of memory. Perhaps this would explain why God allows His people to taste the painful consequences of their disobedience. This is because God desires to create a clear memory of the pain of ignoring the technology of divine interception in the memory banks of His covenant people. This is because God intends to use what is stored in His people's memory banks to excite the technology of divine interception in their future destiny.

> *God desires to create a clear memory of the pain of ignoring the technology of divine interception in the memory banks of His covenant people.*

NATURE

But God shows his anger from heaven against all sinful, wicked people who suppress the truth by their wickedness.[19] They know the truth about God because he has made it obvious to them. [20] For ever since the world was created, people have seen the earth and sky. Through everything God made, they can clearly see his invisible qualities—his eternal power and divine nature. So they have no excuse for not knowing God. Romans 1:18-20

One of the greatest creations of God is the entity called "nature." Before God created nature He could only know Himself, with everything else that He has ever created existing only in His mind. When God created nature He created the possibility of existence for everything else that He wanted to create in nature. Before God created nature, angels, mankind, trees, oceans, mountains, animals, fish, birds and ants only existed as a concept in His mind.

So here is the million dollar question, "What is nature?" "Nature" is the Creator's eternal artistry canvas. Nature is the canvas on which the great artist (God) paints what He has conceived in His mind. Every artist knows that the paintings they have in their mind will remain unrevealed if they are not painted onto a canvas. While Leonardo Davinci's legendary painting of the "Mona Lisa" has inspired millions of art lovers, his famous painting is not a living object. God on the other hand as an artist, is in a class all by Himself.

God is the only artist who can paint what was in His mind onto the canvas of nature and cause His paintings to come to life as well. This is why Paul, the great apostle to the Church, declares all that needs to be known about God is revealed in the canvas of nature. This is why nature is one of God's favorite vehicles of manifesting the technology of divine interception. In this passage I will show you how the great artist uses nature to bring the necessary interception in the lives of His Kingdom citizens.

Arise, go to Nineveh, that great city, and cry against it; for their wickedness is come up before me. ³But Jonah rose up to flee unto Tarshish from the presence of the LORD, and went down to Joppa; and he found a ship going to Tarshish: so he paid the fare thereof, and went down into it, to go with them unto Tarshish from the presence of the LORD. ⁴But the LORD sent out a great wind into the sea, and there was a mighty tempest in the sea, so that the ship was like to be broken. ⁵Then the mariners were afraid, and cried every man unto his god, and cast forth the wares that were in the ship into the sea, to lighten it of them. But Jonah was gone down into the sides of the ship; and he lay, and was fast asleep.
Jonah 1:2-5

Movies have been created to portray the life of the runaway prophet, Jonah. For whatever reason the world has been fascinated by the story of Jonah and how he found himself in the belly of a great fish. Perhaps it is because many of us can identify with Jonah's wayward heart, a heart that is constantly running from God and yet wanting God at the same time. But whatever fascinates you about the story of Jonah, it is one of the most powerful examples of how God uses nature as a vehicle to manifest the technology of divine interception in the affairs of men.

The Bible tells us that Jonah received a prophetic commission from the Lord about the impending judgment of God against the wicked people of Nineveh. But instead of obeying God, Jonah decided to run to a city called Tarshish. While Jonah was on a ship headed in the wrong direction from the will of God, God sent a mighty storm that shook the boat that Jonah was on. God had sent the technology of divine interception through the storm. Nature itself had raised up a storm to intercept the prophet's disobedience to God. We can clearly see from the story how God can use nature to manifest the technology of divine interception.

> *And when the ass saw the angel of the LORD, she fell down under Balaam: and Balaam's anger was kindled, and he smote the ass with a staff. 28And the LORD opened the mouth of the ass, and she said unto Balaam, What have I done unto thee, that thou hast smitten me these three times? 29And Balaam said unto the ass, Because thou hast mocked me: I would there were a sword in mine hand, for now would I kill thee. 30And the ass said unto Balaam, Am not I thine ass, upon which thou hast ridden ever since I was thine unto this day? Was I ever wont to do so unto thee? And he said, Nay. 31Then the LORD opened the eyes of Balaam, and he saw the angel of the LORD standing in the way, and his sword drawn in his hand: and he bowed down his head, and fell flat on his face. 32And the angel of the LORD said unto him, Wherefore hast thou smitten thine ass these three times? Behold, I went out to withstand thee, because thy way is perverse before me: 33And the ass saw me, and turned from me these three times: unless she had turned from me, surely now also I had slain thee, and saved her alive. 34And Balaam said unto the angel of the LORD, I have sinned; for I knew not that thou stoodest in the way against me: now therefore, if it displease thee, I will get me back again. Numbers 22:27-34*

In the book of Numbers we have another incident where God

uses nature to manifest the technology of divine interception. It is a story involving the false prophet by the name of Balaam. This false prophet had been hired by Balak the leader of the Assyrians, to curse the children of Israel. But each time he tried to curse them God gave the false prophet a powerful word of blessing. Any reasonable person would have known that God was against what he was trying to do, but this false prophet was driven by the engines of greed. He wanted the gold more than he wanted God in his life. But the more he tried to curse Israel, the more God gave him words of blessing.

One day when the mad prophet driven by his own greed made an attempt to embark on a journey to go to Balak's camp to curse Israel one more time, God sent an angel to kill the wayward prophet. The angel of the Lord would have killed this rebellious prophet for hire had it not been for the prophet's donkey who saw the angel of the Lord standing in the middle of the road with a flaming sword.

How ironic that the prophet's donkey was more sensitive to the realm of the spirit than the mad prophet. God used the donkey to manifest the technology of divine interception and save the life of the errant prophet. This story, though at times humorous, is embedded with precious nuggets of truth concerning the role that nature plays in manifesting the technology of divine interception. When the spiritual eyes of the mad prophet were finally opened to see the angel of the Lord who was standing in the middle of the road, the angel confessed to the prophet that had it not been for the donkey he would have killed the mercenary prophet. It is clear then that nature is one of the vehicles for manifesting the technology of divine interception in the affairs of men.

NATURAL PARENTS

Those who spare the rod of discipline hate their children. Those who love their children care enough to discipline them. Proverbs 13:24

A youngster's heart is filled with foolishness, but physical discipline will drive it far away. Proverbs 22:15

THE VEHICLES OF DIVINE INTERCEPTION

One of God's favorite vehicles for manifesting the technology of divine interception is our natural parents. Our parents are usually the primary authority figures that God gives us from infancy to adulthood. This is why God uses them to manifest this ancient technology of divine interception. The United States Department of Family Services has sobering statistics that prove that parents are critical pieces in manifesting the technology of divine interception in the lives of their children. Orphans are seven times more likely to end up in jail than children that are raised by a mother and father.

King Solomon had this to say about how natural parents can intercept foolishness in the hearts of their children. In Proverbs 13:24 the wise king tells us that parents who spare the rod of discipline hate their own children. King Solomon was also convinced that physical discipline is the antidote to foolishness in the heart of a child. Looking back, there are a lot of problems that I would have gotten into because of the foolishness of my young heart, had my parents not intercepted much of it. This is why the Lord Jesus admonished children to honor their parents so they could live long lives.

During the 2009 Christmas holidays we almost had another September 11 incident in the United States of America. There was a Nigerian born terrorist who boarded a flight to Michigan intending to blow up the airplane once it landed. This would have certainly been the case had it not been for this terrorist's father who went to the American Embassy in Nigeria to report the intended crime. God used this Nigerian terrorist's natural parents, as well as several passengers on the flight, to intercept the demonic agenda to blow up a plane full of innocent people.

SPIRITUAL COVERING

I am writing to Timothy, my true son in the faith. May God the Father and Christ Jesus our Lord give you grace, mercy, and peace. ³ When I left for Macedonia, I urged you to stay there in Ephesus and stop those whose teaching is contrary to the truth. ⁴ Don't let them waste their time in endless discussion of myths and spiritual pedigrees. These things only lead to meaningless

*speculations, which don't help people live a life of faith in God. 1
Timothy 1:2-4*

Just like there are natural parents, there are also spiritual parents.
Since we are all spirit beings having a bodily experience, spiritual parents
carry a greater assignment than our natural parents do. Our natural parents
have a God-given mandate to nurture us into physical, mental, emotional
and spiritual maturity; however, many natural, adoptive or step-parents
fall short of God's best for their children. Therefore, God provides the
Church with spiritual parents who have a God-given mandate to nurture
His children into spiritual maturity in Christ. Our natural parents show
us how to become useful, productive citizens within our community and
culture, and our spiritual parents teach us how to operate in the economy
of the Kingdom of God. The fortunate few whose natural parents also
function as spiritual parents are doubly blessed.

The apostolic model of having spiritual parents in our lives is
known as spiritual covering. No normal person would dare walk into
the streets naked. The first order of business when normal people wake
up is to put on clothing. These clothes or garments become the covering
to what otherwise would have been a naked body roaming the streets.
Such clothes are our natural covering. Putting on clothes intercepts
the condition of nakedness from being viewed by all. Imagine a very
beautiful woman walking the streets among a cluster of men, while she
is completely naked. She would be a very easy and tempting target for
sexual assault. But if she was properly clothed, the probability of being
sexually assaulted would be highly diminished.

If clothes can provide such an adequate covering that can
intercept many evil events, just imagine how much more evil a spiritual
covering can intercept in the realm of the spirit. The apostle Paul called
Timothy his spiritual son in the faith. This means that Paul was operating
as a spiritual parent to this young apostle. When we observe the life and
ministry of Timothy we can see that Paul's spiritual covering—which
included serving as a role model, mentor and father—intercepted a lot of
demonic activity against this young apostle. Observing the life of young
Timothy gives us insight into how God uses spiritual covering to manifest
the technology of divine interception in the human plane.

THE VEHICLES OF DIVINE INTERCEPTION

In my own journey I have been intercepted several times by God through the ministry and counsel of my spiritual fathers in the faith. It is clear to me that God loves to use spiritual parents and/or spiritual covering to manifest the technology of divine interception in the lives of His children. This is why marketplace leaders must be diligent and prudent to have a proper spiritual covering in place before attempting to invade or take dominion of any of the seven mountains of culture that they feel called to influence or conquer.

THE CONSCIENCE

Cling to your faith in Christ, and keep your conscience clear. For some people have deliberately violated their consciences; as a result, their faith has been shipwrecked. [20] Hymenaeus and Alexander are two examples. I threw them out and handed them over to Satan so they might learn not to blaspheme God. 1 Timothy 1:19-20

In my humble opinion one of the greatest vehicles of the technology of divine interception is a powerful intrusive thing called the conscience. By definition the "conscience" is "the inner sense of what is right or wrong in one's conduct or motives, impending one toward the right action." From this definition we can clearly see that the conscience is like having a very powerful policeman who lives in our head. It does not take a rocket scientist to figure out why God likes to use the conscience as a primary vehicle for manifesting the technology of divine interception in our heads.

The conscience is the inner voice that is usually the first one to tell us not to do what is wrong before we do it. This is why the Scriptures tell us that no human being will be without excuse when they stand before the judgment seat of God. When we stand before the judgment seat of God when our earthly life is over, our conscience will be our greatest ally or our greatest enemy. Paul the Apostle in speaking to his spiritual son Timothy admonishes him to keep his conscience clear. Paul further tells Timothy that people who deliberately violate their conscience have made shipwreck of their faith. Scripture says it is possible for our conscience to become seared, and that in those cases, there remains no more sacrifice for sin. This tells us that ignoring this powerful vehicle of the technology of divine interception is like playing with fire and dabbling in pure foolishness.

Even Gentiles, who do not have God's written law, show that they know his law when they instinctively obey it, even without having heard it. [15] They demonstrate that God's law is written in their hearts, for their own conscience and thoughts either accuse them or tell them they are doing right. [16] And this is the message I proclaim—that the day is coming when God, through Christ Jesus, will judge everyone's secret life. Romans 2:14-16

In his apostolic discourse to the church in Rome, the apostle Paul makes a very strong case for the conscience. He shows us that even the Gentiles who do not have God's written law, show that they know His law when they instinctively obey it without even having heard it. The apostle Paul argues that by so doing the Gentiles prove that God's law is written on the tablets of their hearts, since our own conscience and thoughts either accuse them or tell them what they are doing is right. Do you remember the time when you were caught by your mother with your hands in the cookie jar and you knew you were guilty without your mother having to say so? This is because there was a little voice inside your head that told you not to dip your fingers in the cookie jar without permission. This inner voice is one of the greatest vehicles of the technology of divine interception. I have listened to the horror stories of Kingdom entrepreneurs who lost millions of dollars by ignoring this powerful technology of divine interception through the conscience. May this book put an end to the foolishness of violating the conscience.

They say unto him, Master, this woman was taken in adultery, in the very act. [5]Now Moses in the law commanded us, that such should be stoned: but what sayest thou? [6]This they said, tempting him, that they might have to accuse him. But Jesus stooped down, and with his finger wrote on the ground, as though he heard them not. [7]So when they continued asking him, he lifted up himself, and said unto them, He that is without sin among you, let him first cast a stone at her. [8]And again he stooped down, and wrote on the ground. ⁹And they which heard it, being convicted by their own conscience, went out one by one, beginning at the eldest, even unto the last: and Jesus was left alone, and the woman standing in the midst. John 8:4-9

There are very few things I despise more than the religious spirit. Maybe I'm too much like Jesus Christ, who couldn't stand the hypocritical nature of the religious spirit. Some of the religious leaders brought a woman who was caught in adultery to Jesus Christ. They told Jesus that they had caught the woman in the very act. If you have lived long enough you would have to admit that it is impossible for a woman to commit adultery by herself. If these religious leaders had caught this woman in the very act, what happened to the man she was sleeping with?

I can tell you what happened to the mysterious man. He was probably one of the friends of the religious leaders who was accusing her in the first place. They probably gave him a pass from sin to safeguard his reputation in the community. They did not bring the woman caught in adultery to Jesus because they were passionate about righteousness. The woman was a mere political pawn in their religious conspiracy to entrap Jesus into a theological debacle about the Law of Moses. So the stakes were bigger than just the woman's life, as if that weren't enough. The religious leaders were seeking to discredit Jesus and his ministry in order to justify themselves and their own religious ideology and self-righteous behavior.

But how can the created play mind games against the Creator and win? The Pharisees were in way over the heads with this one. Since they were left standing in front of the Word that created them in the first place, Jesus simply awakened the voice of their conscience and intercepted their diabolical religious conspiracy against him. Without lifting his head, while he drew on the ground, Jesus challenged the Pharisees to stone her if they were not guilty of sin themselves. What happened next would have made headline news for primetime television. The Scriptures declare that one by one, all of the men who came to accuse this woman before Jesus dropped their stones and walked away from the oldest to the youngest.

What led to such an amazing turnaround of events? What happened to this woman's passionate accusers? Why did they drop their stones of accusation and leave the woman with Jesus with their tails hanging between their legs? The Bible says they were convicted by the voice of their own conscience which unmasked their sinful lifestyle. Essentially Jesus used their conscience as a vehicle of manifesting the technology of divine interception in order to deliver this poor woman from their diabolical conspiracy. Had it not been for the conscience acting as a vehicle for the technology of divine interception, this poor woman who was caught in adultery would have been stoned to death to satisfy the bloated and insatiable religious egos and appetites of these hypocrites. Thank God for divine interception because she lived to see another day, and hopefully learned from her near death experience and the love and mercy shown to her by Jesus to live a godly and productive life.

PAIN

The Israelites did evil in the LORD's sight. So the LORD handed them over to the Midianites for seven years. ² The Midianites were so cruel that the Israelites made hiding places for themselves in the mountains, caves, and strongholds. ⁶ So Israel was reduced to starvation by the Midianites. Then the Israelites cried out to the LORD for help. ⁷ When they cried out to the LORD because of Midian, ⁸ the LORD sent a prophet to the Israelites. He said, "This is what the LORD, the God of Israel, says: I brought you up out of slavery in Egypt. ⁹ I rescued you from the Egyptians and from all who oppressed you. I drove out your enemies and gave you their land. ¹⁰ I told you, 'I am the LORD your God. You must not worship the gods of the Amorites, in whose land you now live.' But you have not listened to me."Judges 6:1-2, 7-10

There are very few things that are as powerful as pain. This is because no one that is healthy likes to feel pain. We were all created to gravitate toward pleasure. This is why most human beings run away from or avoid situations that can inflict or cause pain. But if the truth is told, pain is not really an enemy; it serves merely to prove that one does exist. When there is pain in a marriage or other relationship – or even in our physical bodies – it is indicative of the fact that something that should be in order is already out of order. It is really the misalignment of orderly parts that creates pain in any relationship or in any business venture.

Since pain is an indicator that an enemy does exist, we should really embrace moments of pain when they come. We should mine these moments of pain out of all the nuggets of truth that we can pluck out of any given situation in order to accurately discern the source of our pain. It is in the discernment of the source of our pain that pain truly becomes a powerful vehicle of manifesting the technology of divine interception.

One of the benefits of tithing under the Order of Melchizedek that I have taught my church is the benefit of tithing for the manifestation of the technology of divine interception. Consequently, many of the people in our church when they give tithes do so believing that God would reward them with moments of divine interception. A couple of months ago, one of our pastors in the church began to experience great difficulty in being able to speak normally. While he was in one of our services he felt a tingling sensation go through his body. Seeing the intensity of the pain that her husband was going through, his wife insisted that he see a doctor right away. Reluctantly he made an appointment to see the doctor. When he got to the hospital he was quickly ushered into the intensive care unit and the medical professionals were surprised he was still walking because all the science pointed to the fact that he should have already been dead.

The doctors discovered that he was diabetic and the sugar levels in his bloodstream had skyrocketed to an unbelievable number. Had he waited any longer than he did the doctors said that he would have died that same day. This is why I maintain that pain is not really an enemy but a warning mechanism that God has wisely created to interface with our physical bodies, emotions, spirits and in human relationships to expose the covert activities of a more sinister enemy who opposes our life's calling and assignments. What I have observed over the years from studying human behavior, is that our genius for solution seems to emerge prominently whenever we are determined to eliminate what is causing us pain. It is the testament of human history that some of the most powerful scientific breakthroughs and technological advancements came as a result of pain.

THE WISDOM OF GOD

There was a small town with only a few people, and a great king came with his army and besieged it. ¹⁵ *A poor, wise man knew how to save the town, and so it was rescued. But afterward no one thought to thank him.* ¹⁶ *So even though wisdom is better than strength, those who are wise will be despised if they are poor. What they say will not be appreciated for long. Ecclesiastes 9:14-16*

In my humble opinion the greatest vehicle of the technology of divine interception is the wisdom of God. There is nothing on the human plane that is higher than the wisdom of God. Perhaps this is the reason why King Solomon became the richest king who has ever lived because he was given the gift of the wisdom of God. Ecclesiastes 9:14-16 tells us the story of a small town that was surrounded by a king with a great army. The military might of the small town was no match for the king who surrounded the city, but the small town was delivered from the power of the great king because one poor man was anointed with the wisdom of God. This poor man's wisdom became the vehicle of the technology of divine interception. It is no wonder King Solomon says that a companion of fools shall be destroyed.

Some time later two prostitutes came to the king to have an argument settled. ¹⁷ *"Please, my lord," one of them began, "this woman and I live in the same house. I gave birth to a baby while she was with me in the house.* ¹⁸ *Three days later this woman also had a baby. We were alone; there were only two of us in the house.* ¹⁹ *"But her baby died during the night when she rolled over on it.* ²⁰ *Then she got up in the night and took my son from beside me while I was asleep. She laid her dead child in my arms and took mine to sleep beside her.* ²¹ *And in the morning when I tried to nurse my son, he was dead! But when I looked more closely in the morning light, I saw that it wasn't my son at all."* ²² *Then the other woman interrupted, "It certainly was your son, and the living child is mine." "No," the first woman said, "the living child is mine, and the dead one is yours." And so they argued back and forth before the king.* ²³ *Then the king said, "Let's get the facts straight. Both of you claim the living child is yours, and each says that the dead one belongs to the other.* ²⁴ *All right, bring me a sword." So a sword was brought to the king.* ²⁵ *Then he said, "Cut the living child in two, and give half to one woman and half to the other!"* ²⁶ *Then the woman who was the real mother of the living child, and who loved him very much, cried out, "Oh no, my lord! Give her the child—please do not kill him!" But the other woman said, "All right, he will be neither yours nor mine; divide him between us!"* ²⁷ *Then the king said, "Do not kill the child, but give him to the woman who wants him to live, for she is his mother!"* ²⁸ *When all Israel heard the king's decision, the people were in awe of the king, for they saw the wisdom God had given him for rendering justice. 1 Kings 3:16-28*

One of the greatest Bible stories that has intrigued and fascinated millions of listeners is the story of the two prostitutes that came before King Solomon. This was just after King Solomon was crowned king of the nation of Israel. As the story goes these two prostitutes gave birth to two healthy babies. But one of the prostitutes got careless in her sleep and slept on top of her newborn baby. As the night progressed into the morning hours the prostitute who suffocated her baby woke up and realized what she had done.

To remedy the situation she took the body of her dead baby and placed it under the arms of the other prostitute whose baby was still alive. She then took the living baby and placed it under her arms. When the light of day broke into the house where these two prostitutes were sleeping, the mother of the living baby knew that she had been deceived. She knew that the dead baby under her arms was not hers. A serious custody battle broke out between the two prostitutes concerning who had custody rights to the living baby.

The two women were eventually brought before King Solomon who was given the task of judging their case. As soon as they got into the king's presence the two prostitutes began to fight bitterly over who had custodial rights to the living baby. Since there was no DNA or paternity tests in those days the king needed the wisdom of God to judge these two prostitutes righteously and accurately. King Solomon then did something very unconventional. He told one of his bodyguards to cut the living baby in half and give one half of the baby's body to one woman and the other half to the other woman.

The woman who had actually killed her baby during sleep, gloated in the king's judgment. She was passionately encouraging the king's swordsman to cut the baby in half. But the mother of the living baby was in distress at the prospect of seeing the baby cut in half. So she begged the king not to cut the baby in half but instead give the living baby to the other woman. When the king saw compassion for the baby he knew she was the true mother of the living baby. In a stunning reversal of fortune, the king ruled that the living baby should be given to its true mother. The king through the wisdom of God had intercepted a diabolical conspiracy to destroy an innocent baby by an evil and calculating woman. This powerful biblical story proves that the wisdom of God is one of the most powerful vehicles of manifesting the technology of divine interception in human affairs.

LIFE APPLICATION SECTION

MEMORY VERSE

For there are three that bear record in heaven, the Father, the Word, and the Holy Ghost: and these three are one. 1 John 5:7

REFLECTIONS

Explain why the Godhead is such a powerful vehicle of the Technology of Divine Interception?

_____

_____

_____

_____

_____

_____

Explain why Prophets are such a powerful vehicle of the Technology of Divine Interception?

_____

_____

_____

_____

_____

_____

JOURNAL YOUR THOUGHTS

THE VEHICLES OF DIVINE INTERCEPTION

CHAPTER TWELVE
THE FRUIT OF DIVINE INTERCEPTION

In this chapter I will take some time to celebrate the stories of the men and women of the Bible who allowed God to intercept them and were the better for it, along with the people they influenced. I want you to celebrate the fruit of the technology of divine interception.

WIDOW OF SIDON

Then the LORD said to Elijah, [9] "Go and live in the village of Zarephath, near the city of Sidon. I have instructed a widow there to feed you." So he went to Zarephath. As he arrived at the gates of the village, he saw a widow gathering sticks, and he asked her, "Would you please bring me a little water in a cup?" [11] As she was going to get it, he called to her, "Bring me a bite of bread, too." [12] But she said, "I swear by the LORD your God that I don't have a single piece of bread in the house. And I have only a handful of flour left in the jar and a little cooking oil in the bottom of the jug. I was just gathering a few sticks to cook this last meal, and then my son and I will die." ¹³ But Elijah said to her, "Don't be afraid! Go ahead and do just what you've said, but make a little bread for me first. Then use what's left to prepare a meal for yourself and your son. ¹⁴ For this is what the LORD, the God of Israel, says: There will always be flour and olive oil left in your containers until the time when the LORD sends rain and the crops grow again!" ¹⁵ So she did as Elijah said, and she and Elijah and her son continued to eat for many days. ¹⁶ There was always enough flour and olive oil left in the containers, just as the LORD had promised through Elijah. 1 Kings 17:8-15

When the prophet Elijah entered the gates of the city of Sidon, there was a widow woman who was gathering sticks at the gates to the city. Little did she know that she was about to be intercepted. Her whole life was about to change completely through the spirit of divine interception. Even though life had not been fair to her, things were about to change radically for the better.

Even though she had lost much and was deeply impoverished, God was about to intercept something that was in her possession which was connected to her future. Even though she was despondent about her desperate circumstances, she was about to make a decision that would have sentenced her to a lifetime of poverty. She was at the city gates gathering sticks to make her final meal. The only problem is that what she was fixing to eat was not her harvest; it was her "seed" for a more prosperous future.

But God sent one of his choicest prophets to intercept her action of wanting to eat her "SEED" instead of "SOWING IT" for a supernatural bumper harvest. Elijah was sent to her as a vehicle of the technology of divine interception to intercept her seed. When she responded in obedience to the technology of divine interception, God blessed her to such an extent that the cruse of oil and the jar of meal in her house never diminished. God supernaturally took her out of the recession that was affecting everybody else around her. She lived in abundance for the rest of the famine.

> *One of the most dramatic stories involving the fruit of divine interception is the story of the prophet Jonah.*

JONAH'S STORY

Then the LORD spoke to Jonah a second time: ² "Get up and go to the great city of Nineveh, and deliver the message I have given you." ³ This time Jonah obeyed the LORD's command and went to Nineveh, a city so large that it took three days to see it all. ⁴ On the day Jonah entered the city, he shouted to the crowds: "Forty days from now Nineveh will be destroyed!" ⁵ The people of Nineveh believed God's message, and from the greatest to the least, they declared a fast and put on burlap to show their sorrow. ⁶ When the king of Nineveh heard what Jonah was saying, he stepped down from his throne and took off his royal robes. He dressed himself in burlap and sat on a heap of ashes. ⁷ Then the king and his nobles sent this decree throughout the city: "No one, not even the animals from your herds and flocks, may eat or drink anything at all. ⁸ People and animals alike must wear garments of mourning, and everyone must pray earnestly to God. They must turn from their evil ways and stop all their violence. ⁹ Who can tell? Perhaps even yet God will change his mind and hold back his fierce anger from destroying us." ¹⁰ When God saw what they had done and how they had put a stop to their evil ways, he changed his mind and did not carry out the destruction he had threatened. Jonah 3:1-10

Perhaps one of the most dramatic stories involving the fruit of divine interception is the story of the prophet Jonah. Jonah started out as an unwilling prophet who did not want to obey God or go to the land of Nineveh. So the shaky prophet jumped into a ship that was headed in the opposite direction from where God was sending him to. God sent a storm at sea that was threatening to capsize the ship that Jonah was in. Even the owners of the ship knew that there was something extraordinary about this particular storm, so they cast lots to determine who had angered the gods.

As fate would have it, the lots fell on Jonah. The men of the ship turned to Jonah with an accusing look and asked him why the gods were after him. Jonah confessed that he was a prophet of the living God who was running away from his prophetic assignment. At Jonah's request they threw him overboard and the stormed stopped immediately. Once Jonah's body touched the water he was swallowed by a big fish almost immediately.

After Jonah repented of his attitude and began to respond positively to the technology of divine interception, God told the fish to spit him out in Nineveh. Once he arrived in Nineveh, Jonah began to preach up a storm telling the inhabitants of the land that God would destroy them within forty days. When the king of Nineveh heard the content of Jonah's message he was deeply moved. He immediately got off his throne and went into a fast of mourning.

The king of Nineveh sent out a decree through his nobles that every one in Nineveh had to repent to God in sackcloth and ashes. The king was so serious about this fast on national repentance that he even made the animals fast for a whole day. God was so moved by this king's heartfelt repentance that He stayed His hand of judgment. Jonah's reluctant message had saved an entire nation. The fruit of this moment of divine interception is forever forged into the annals of human history.

JOSEPH'S STORY

"Please, come closer," he said to them. So they came closer. And he said again, "I am Joseph, your brother, whom you sold into slavery in Egypt. ⁵ But don't be upset, and don't be angry with yourselves for selling me to this place. It was God who sent me here ahead of you to preserve your lives. ⁶ This famine that has ravaged the land for two years will last five more years, and there will be neither plowing nor harvesting. ⁷ God has sent me ahead of you to keep you and your families alive and to preserve many

survivors. [8] So it was God who sent me here, not you! And he is the one who made me an adviser to Pharaoh—the manager of his entire palace and the governor of all Egypt. [9] "Now hurry back to my father and tell him, 'This is what your son Joseph says: God has made me master over all the land of Egypt. So come down to me immediately! [10] You can live in the region of Goshen, where you can be near me with all your children and grandchildren, your flocks and herds, and everything you own. [11] I will take care of you there, for there are still five years of famine ahead of us. Otherwise you, your household, and all your animals will starve.'" Genesis 45:4-11

The story of Joseph, the young and unpretentious Jewish boy who was sold into a life of slavery by his own brothers, who later became the most powerful man in Egypt, rhymes with divine romance. How can such a sad story capture the imagination of millions of people around the world and in every dispensation? I believe the answer lies in the fact that Joseph's story belies our inherent desire to be intercepted by God so that our latter years can be better than our former.

When Joseph was released out of prison by Pharaoh's guards to go and interpret the dreams of the king of Egypt little did he know that his purpose for being in Egypt was about to be revealed in a very dramatic fashion. After Pharaoh finished recounting his dream to Joseph, Joseph was stunned by the prophetic implications of Pharaoh's dream. Suddenly the purpose behind everything that he had been through became as clear as crystal.

He realized right there and then, that it was not his brother's jealousy that brought him to Egypt but it was "the spirit of divine interception." Joseph realized in the twinkling of an eye that he was a recipient and vehicle of God's interception technology. He realized then that God had sent him to help during the worst famine in recorded human history. When his brothers arrived at his doorsteps in search of food it became stunningly clear to him that what they had meant for evil God had meant for good through interception technology.

When Joseph was able to move his entire family into the best land in

Egypt (Goshen) during the worst economic recession in recorded human history, he saw firsthand the fruit of divine interception. Joseph could see without a shadow of a doubt that had he not been sent ahead of his family by God to intercept the effects of the famine, his entire family would have been wiped out by starvation. I am sure Joseph was thankful that he was an ambassador under a Kingdom that is serviced by the most powerful interception technology in all of creation.

THE SHUNAMITE WOMAN

During the course of this writing, we have stated that prophets are often used by God as vehicles of divine interception. This is why the Bible says that the Lord God will do nothing except he reveals His secrets to His servants the prophets (Amos 3:7). Without a doubt, there are many stories of divine interception in the Bible involving prophets, but very few have captured my imagination and showcase the benefits of responding to the technology of divine interception like this story of the Shunammite woman.

> *Joseph realized in the twinkling of an eye that he was a recipient and vehicle of God's interception technology.*

THE INTERCEPTION

Elisha had told the woman whose son he had brought back to life, "Take your family and move to some other place, for the LORD has called for a famine on Israel that will last for seven years." ² So the woman did as the man of God instructed. She took her family and settled in the land of the Philistines for seven years. 2 Kings 8:1-2

What is striking about this story is that the Shunammite was a woman of great means. She and her family were very wealthy. They had deep and serious investments in the community they lived in. This meant that migration for them was a very difficult process. If anybody had an excuse for staying put, it was this woman and her family. They had serious and deep investments in the community that tied them to the community. But she also knew by experience the dangers of ignoring the technology of divine interception. She moved on her husband and household and made them migrate to a foreign country in obedience to the prophet of God. This woman was determined to cooperate with the technology of divine interception.

I am sure that when this woman and her husband announced they were migrating to a foreign country and abandoning all of their investments in the community, their friends and extended family probably laughed at them. And to top it off, their radical decision was based upon a prophetic warning from a bald headed prophet. But the Shunammite woman was willing to endure the scorn, ridicule and mockery of her friends rather than disobey the technology of divine interception. History would later prove her right.

THE FRUIT OF OBEDIENCE

After the famine ended she returned from the land of the Philistines, and she went to see the king about getting back her house and land. ⁴ As she came in, the king was talking with Gehazi, the servant of the man of God. The king had just said, "Tell me some stories about the great things Elisha has done." ⁵ And Gehazi was telling the king about the time Elisha had brought a boy back to life. At that very moment, the mother of the boy walked in to make her appeal to the king about her house and land. "Look, my lord the king!" Gehazi exclaimed. "Here is the woman now, and this is her son—the very one Elisha brought back to life!" ⁶ "Is this true?" the king asked her. And she told him the story. So he directed one of his officials to see that everything she had lost was restored to her, including the value of any crops that had been

THE FRUIT OF DIVINE INTERCEPTION

harvested during her absence. 2 Kings 8:1-6

The Shunammite woman and her family lived in exile for a period of seven years in accordance with the prophetic word of the prophet of God. While they were in exile, a serious famine struck the land and community that they used to live in just like the prophet had said. In the eighth year the woman and her family returned to the land of their Nativity in accordance with the word of the man of God.

The timing of her return to her native country could not have been more perfect. The Bible tells us that on the day she returned to her native country the king was investigating the powerful ministry of the prophet Elisha. He had invited Gehazi, Elisha's servant of many years, to tell him about his firsthand accounts of the miracles of God that he witnessed when he was working for this mighty prophet of God. Gehazi was more than happy to oblige. While he was telling the king about how God had used the prophet Elisha to raise a boy who had died, the Shunammite woman and her family just happened to enter the courts of the king's palace at that exact moment. When Gehazi saw her he was very excited, because he knew that she could collaborate his story before the king.

Gehazi pointed to her and told the king that this was the woman whose child Elisha had raised from the dead. Gehazi also told the king that the young man standing next to her was in actuality, the boy who was raised from the dead by the great prophet. The king was visibly moved by this miraculous story to such an extent that he was willing to do anything before God to restore the lost fortunes of the Shunammite woman. He gave her back her land and properties. In addition, the king told his treasurer to calculate what this woman should have had, had she been able to harvest her land for the past seven years that she was in exile. When the king's treasurer was able to calculate the actual amount, the king gave it to her. This woman experienced firsthand the fruit of obeying the technology of divine interception.

> *I realized that I had become addicted to divine intervention. I had officially become a deliverance junkie. I was addicted to drama instead of peace.*

WHAT IS YOUR STORY

So what is your story? Have you at some point in your journey with God experienced the benefits of obeying his voice before you had the evidence for doing so? It is my heartfelt prayer that this book has placed in your heart a burning desire to become a champion at cooperating with the technology of divine interception. I don't know about you but I'm tired of going through a life of endless drama. I have had more than my fair share of going from one crisis to the next and believing God to intervene in each one. I am so ready to live a life that is governed not by drama, but by the spirit of divine interception. I got so tired of hearing the fire trucks rushing to my house because my house was on fire again. I realized that I had become addicted to divine intervention. I had officially become a deliverance junkie. I was addicted to drama instead of peace and thought divine intervention was proof that the favor of God was upon my life.

DIVINE INTERCEPTION: OUR BIRTHRIGHT

A dear friend and business partner of mine, Dr. Breakthrough (Stan Harris) told me that when he first heard me teach on the difference between divine intervention and divine interception, God talked and gave him revelation in the spirit. God told him that divine interception was the birthright of his children, not divine intervention. He also realized that he had talked with a couple of teenagers who were raised in a God-fearing home, who felt like they could not minister to anybody because they did not have the testimonies of drama and ongoing crisis that they saw glorified in the church world. He told me, "Dr. Myles, I am going to go back to these teenagers and tell them that they have the best testimonies in the house of God because theirs is a testimony of divine interception, as opposed to testimonies of divine intervention." I could not agree more. Our children do not have to become addicted to drugs and then have God deliver them before they can say they have a godly testimony.

LIFE APPLICATION SECTION

MEMORY VERSE

Then the Lord *spoke to Jonah a second time:* [2] *"Get up and go to the great city of Nineveh, and deliver the message I have given you."* [3] *This time Jonah obeyed the* Lord*'s command and went to Nineveh, a city so large that it took three days to see it all,* [4] *On the day Jonah entered the city, he shouted to the crowds: "Forty days from now Nineveh will be destroyed!"* [5] *The people of Nineveh believed God's message, and from the greatest to the least, they declared a fast and put on burlap to show their sorrow.* [6] *When the king of Nineveh heard what Jonah was saying, he stepped down from his throne and took off his royal robes. He dressed himself in burlap and sat on a heap of ashes.* [7] *Then the king and his nobles sent this decree throughout the city: "No one, not even the animals from your herds and flocks, may eat or drink anything at all.* [8] *People and animals alike must wear garments of mourning, and everyone must pray earnestly to God. They must turn from their evil ways and stop all their violence.* [9] *Who can tell? Perhaps even yet God will change his mind and hold back his fierce anger from destroying us."* [10] *When God saw what they had done and how they had put a stop to their evil ways, he changed his mind and did not carry out the destruction he had threatened. Jonah 3:1-10*

REFLECTIONS

What does this phrase mean to you "the Fruit of Divine Interception?"

_____

_____

_____

_____

_____

_____

What happened to the Shunammite woman when she obeyed the Technology of Divine Interception?

_____

_____

_____

_____

_____

_____

THE FRUIT OF DIVINE INTERCEPTION

JOURNAL YOUR THOUGHTS

CHAPTER THIRTEEN
THE CROSS: THE GREATEST
INSTRUMENT OF DIVINE INTERCEPTION

*Then Jesus said to his disciples, "If any of you wants to be my follower, you must turn from your selfish ways, take up your **cross** (emphasis added), and follow me." Matthew 16:24*

> *Through the corridors of human history, especially religious history, nothing has captivated the hearts of men worldwide like the cross of Christ.*

Through the corridors of human history, especially religious history, nothing has captivated the hearts of men worldwide like the cross of Christ. To millions of people of faith from around the world the cross is held in high esteem. The cross has come to symbolize the ultimate sacrifice of the Son of God for a sinful and dying world. But the cross of Christ also attracts demonically engineered spiritual attacks from those who believe that there is no God.

As Scripture says in 1 Corinthians 1:18, "For the message of the cross is foolishness to those who are perishing, but to us who are being saved, it is the power of God."

The passionate and religious obsession with the cross of Christ demands further introspective investigation into this spiritual phenomenon. In the spirit of informed investigation, it behooves us to ask the following questions.

- Why are millions of people of faith drawn in awe to the symbol of the cross?

- Why does the symbol of the cross attract some of the most vicious demonically engineered attacks by atheists?

- Why is the cross of Christ so powerful?

The answer is staggeringly simple, but has far reaching spiritual ramifications. The reason the cross inspires millions of people of faith has a lot to do with how Christ's death transformed an ordinary instrument of death and torture into a steadfast vehicle of the technology of divine interception. Before Jesus died on the cross, the cross was merely an instrument of torture that was used by the Romans to punish those who committed heinous crimes and treason against the empire.

But when Christ willingly offered His life to atone for the sins of the world on the cross, everything changed. The cross went from being a dreaded instrument of torture to becoming the most powerful vehicle of manifesting the technology of divine interception. It is my heartfelt belief that the cross of Christ has become the most powerful instrument for initiating the technology of divine interception. The Bible says, "And having disarmed the powers and authorities, he [Jesus] made a public spectacle of them, triumphing over them by the cross" (Col. 2:15). The cross became a symbol of victory instead of defeat. God turned the tables.

Interestingly enough the first human being to experience the powerful interception technology of the cross of Christ was one of the thieves who was crucified with Him. Before Jesus gave up the ghost, one of the thieves asked Jesus to remember him when He came into paradise. While hanging from the cross, Jesus told the thief who had asked him that they would be together in paradise that very night. This thief went from being hell bound to being heaven bound in the twinkling of an eye. This is the redemptive power that God in his mercy has invested in the cross of Christ—a rich source and treasure trove of interception technology.

THE "PRE-EMPTIVE" POWER

OF THE BLOOD OF CHRIST

Perhaps the most powerful element of divine interception as a pre-emptive technology is found in the fact that God provided salvation and redemption for the human race long before the existence of mankind or the entrance of sin in the Garden of Eden. Often, the issue of redemption is addressed as if Christ's death on the cross was the *"solution"* to an act of sin committed by Adam and Eve. It was just that, but it was also more than that. The infinite wisdom and intelligence of God is the *"fuel"* behind all pre-emptive technology. So, God did know that Adam and Eve would sin, and that the entrance of sin into the human race would require a solution. And, that solution was realized through the death, burial and resurrection of Jesus Christ. However, we must look further into the eternal *"foresight"* of God to see the pre-emptive nature of Christ's sacrifice.

"Searching what, or what manner of time the Spirit of Christ which was in them did signify, when it testified beforehand the sufferings of Christ, and the glory that should follow." 1 Peter 1:11 KJV

The sufferings of Christ were predetermined by the foreknowledge and counsel of an infinitely intelligent God. Because of this predetermined act, there is a *"glory"* that should follow. This *"glory"* is not only the evident redemption of our souls from sin but the active technology of interception that we will come to enjoy and benefit from.

> *"For as much as ye know that ye were not redeemed with corruptible things, as silver and gold, from your vain conversation received by tradition from your fathers; But with the precious blood of Christ, as of a lamb without blemish and without spot: Who verily was foreordained before the foundation of the world, but was manifest in these last times for you."* 1 Peter 1:18-20 KJV

The key word in this text is "foreordained," which is taken from the Greek term "Proginosko" meaning: "Pro," or in front of, prior to, superior to and above; and "Ginosko," meaning: To allow, be aware of, perceive, be resolved, and to understand.

The fact that the redemptive work of Christ was "foreordained" by God gives it the air of sovereignty that is needed to pre-empt the long term results of sin. The power behind ALL pre-emptive technology is the "Foreordained" will and purpose of God! Sin, as potent as it was against the human race, began its course among men, but it was already discovered and destroyed by the infinite foresight of God. Its arrival among the human race was a "doomed expedition" that would ultimately fail to destroy God's divine plan for mankind to rule the earth as He had originally planned. God's perspective on the "sin" issue was addressed by foreordaining the ultimate sacrifice of sinless blood to serve as the solution for mankind.

The power of the blood sacrifice is made available and *"manifest in these last times"* to institute a state of *"reversal"* that literally pre-empts sin from having the final say against us who have chosen to accept Christ as Lord and Savior. This opportunity does not come based simply upon our discovery of the truth, but is *"retroactive"* to the time in which God established His *"foreordained"* plan of redemption. And while we accept the plan of redemption based on the time that we first hear the Gospel and receive Christ into our lives, it was actually a work that was accomplished long before we heard the gospel.

To fully grasp the value of this "pre-emptive strike or technology" against sin we will look at 1 John 2:2.

"And he is the propitiation for our sins: and not for ours only, but also for the whole world."

The term *"Propitiation"* is a multi-faceted word that shows us the great lengths that God has gone through to provide us with a *"win-win"* scenario. Even after we were born in sin and controlled by it, leading up to the time of our salvation, we now have the opportunity to revert back to our *"pre-sin"* state of existence. This is the essence of divine interception technology. We are released from both the crime of our sins and the offense that is produced by our sins against God. *"Propitiation"* is a *"pre-emptive"* technology because it interrupts the long term effect of sin against the human race! The term *"Propitiation"* is taken from the Greek word "Hilasmos," meaning: Atonement and expiation. This means that we are released from BOTH the ***crime*** and the ***offense caused by sin****!* And, if God Himself be for us, who can be against us? But, there is one who tries to attack us with our past! Even after God has released us from the bondage of sin, there is an *"accuser"* who attempts to *"re-install"* the power of sin against us. But, *"Propitiation"* silences the voice of the *"Accuser of the brethren!"* This accuser is not seeking to accuse the sinner; he is trying to accuse the *"brethren."* These are the believers, the ones who are already released from the penalty of sin.

Before the devil can accuse us, we are released from both the crime and the offense! Revelation 12:10 says…

And I heard a loud voice saying in heaven, Now is come salvation, and strength, and the kingdom of our God, and the power of his Christ: for the accuser of our brethren is cast down, which accused them before our God day and night."(KJV)

All accusations are disarmed and intercepted beforehand through *salvation, strength, the Kingdom of God and the power of Christ!* But what makes the cross of Christ so potent in manifesting the technology of divine interception is that it became the center of God's interception technology when Jesus was crucified on it.

THE CROSS: THE GREATEST INSTRUMENT OF DIVINE INTERCEPTION

THE CROSS OF CHRIST AND THE

POWER OF THE LASER BEAM

At the beginning of this chapter I made a very important statement that I want to substantiate at this point. I said that the "Cross of Christ" is the most powerful instrument of divine interception in human history. Why is this? It is due to the fact that the cross by itself has no power to intercept anything. Before Christ died on the cross in total obedience to God the cross was merely an instrument of death and torture. The Babylonians used it to crucify those who committed capital offenses. But it was the mighty Roman Empire that popularized the cross as the most dreaded form of torture. The very mention of the cross struck fear in the hearts of even the most vicious of thieves.

> *The "Cross of Christ" is the most powerful instrument of divine interception in human history.*

But when God put on flesh and chose to die on the cross to redeem all mankind, the meaning of the cross went through a radical transformation. It became the recipient of God's concentrated power as God beamed all the sins of the world from the cradle of civilization till the end of time onto the sinless body of the Son of God who hung on the cross.

The cross of Christ became a recipient of the secret of the laser beam. The secret of the laser beam is concentration. The laser beam releases "concentrated energy" from one main source. It is this concentration of light which helps the laser beam break through some of the most impregnable and resistant substances. One of the latest forms of cancer treatment is proton therapy, where a specialized laser beam is used effectively to treat cancerous tumors or tissues in a less invasive manner than other treatment modalities. When Christ took on the sin of the world and the power of the devil on the cross, the cross received this divine deposit of concentrated light which can penetrate the most impregnable hearts. The cross in that instant became the most powerful instrument or vehicle for manifesting the technology of divine interception.

LIFE APPLICATION SECTION

MEMORY VERSE

*Then Jesus said to his disciples, "If any of you wants to be my follower, you must turn from your selfish ways, take up your **cross** (emphasis added), and follow me. Matthew 16:24*

REFLECTIONS

Why is the "Cross of Christ" held in awe by people of faith?

_____

_____

_____

_____

_____

_____

How did the cross become a powerful instrument of Interception?

_____

_____

_____

_____

_____

_____

THE CROSS: THE GREATEST INSTRUMENT OF DIVINE INTERCEPTION

JOURNAL YOUR THOUGHTS

CHAPTER FOURTEEN
INTERCEPTING THE TOWER OF
BABEL IN HIS CHURCH

This chapter is probably one of the most important chapters in this whole book - so much that I felt this chapter deserved the combined insights of two apostolic voices. So I asked my dear friend Dr. Bruce Cook, apostolic founder of K.E.Y.S- Kingdom Economic Yearly Summit, Leander, Texas to co-author this intrinsic chapter with me. This chapter was born out of our combined apostolic contemplation and prayer. We asked God to help us handle the subject of this chapter with the prayerful and surgical sensitivity that it truly deserves. We both hope and pray that when you read this chapter you will sense that we gave it our best effort.

In my humble opinion one of the greatest divine interceptions in human history (after the cross) is the supernatural interception of the building of the Tower of Babel. This is because this event involved the supernatural interception of the entire human race. From the cradle of civilization God in His creative genius and inner workings of His eternal purpose predetermined that man was created to subdue the earth by establishing God's invisible Kingdom on this physical planet. God's primary divine agenda was to superimpose the governing influence of His

217

invisible Kingdom over our planet. It was not God's plan for mankind to dwell in one specific geographical location. God wanted them to spread their wings and their lineage across the seven continents. But because of the technology of sin and death, which was operating in the spiritual matrix of the human genome, demonic powers began to intercept the divine agenda for the human race.

At one time all the people of the world spoke the same language and used the same words. ² *As the people migrated to the east, they found a plain in the land of Babylonia and settled there.* ³ *They began saying to each other, "Let's make bricks and harden them with fire." (In this region bricks were used instead of stone, and tar was used for mortar.)* ⁴ *Then they said, "Come, let's build a great city for ourselves with a tower that reaches into the sky. This will make us famous and keep us from being scattered all over the world." Genesis 11:1-4*

The devil, in his attempt to overthrow God's plan to advance His invisible Kingdom, raised his own general by the name of Nimrod. Nimrod was a man who was dedicated to the service of demonic powers. He was the great-grandson of Noah, grandson of Ham, and son of Cush. This man had such a powerful spirit of control and manipulation over the souls of men to such an extent that the Bible calls him "a mighty hunter before the Lord." The only problem with his hunting methods was that he was not hunting wild animals; he was a hunter of the souls of men. Nimrod was a personification of the devil because the devil is also a hunter of the souls of men. Nimrod exercised high-level witchcraft over the souls of men. As the self-appointed leader of the entire human race of that era, he forced them to abandon God's will in order to serve a demonic agenda. Nimrod built a global demonic coalition to build a demonic Tower that was going to reach into the heavens. The only problem with this demonic agenda and Nimrod's desire for global domination, making a name for himself, and creating a personal legacy is that it directly contradicted God's eternal mandate for creating the species called man.

But the LORD came down to look at the city and the tower the people were building. ⁶ *"Look!" he said. "The people are united, and they all speak the same language. After this, nothing they set out to do will be impossible for them!* [7] *Come, let's go down and confuse the people with different languages. Then they won't be able to understand each other."* [8] *In that way, the LORD scattered them all over the world, and they stopped building the city. Genesis 11:5-8*

The Bible tells us that God took one look at the Tower that the sons of men were building in a spirit of humanism, pride and rebellion to His revealed will for their lives and decided to act quickly. God came down to the earth and confused the language of the sons of men. Before God confused their language all the people of the earth shared one language. In order to stop the demonic agenda which was gathering momentum over the sons of men, only two generations removed from the flood, God released His interception technology into their common language.

> *In my humble opinion the greatest interception in human history (after the cross) is the supernatural interception of the building of the Tower of Babel.*

God's interception technology released a divine virus in satanic databases and cut off interpersonal communications on the human level. Nimrod's quest to build a demonic tower that would serve as a bridge between heaven and earth came to an abrupt end. Unable to understand each other's language, Nimrod's global coalition disintegrated into tribal factions that scattered.

When God told me to write this book, I had no idea that I would have a chapter in this book titled "Intercepting the Tower of Babel in His Church." I remember how this chapter came to me like it happened yesterday. I was driving to Fort Worth, Texas to the TV recording studios of a dear friend and spiritual protégé of mine. We were going to be recording a series of TV shows for our *The Kingdom in the Marketplace TV Talk Show* when God dropped a powerful revelation in my spirit. Here is what God told me: *"Son, I want to intercept the Tower of Babel in my Church that is hindering the advancement of my Kingdom in the earth."*

This revelation hit me like a deer in headlights. I had never associated the Tower of Babel with the Church. How can God intercept the Tower of Babel in His church, I asked myself. How did the Tower of Babel get into His church in the first place, I continued to ask myself. I was completely captivated by what God had just told me. So I told the Lord to tell me what He meant. Here is what God told me, *"Son, the Tower of Babel is a demonic technology and philosophy which conditions my people to abandon the advancement of my Kingdom in the Earth, in favor of coming up to Heaven."*

Suddenly I saw it as clear as day. In Genesis 11, God was intercepting a demonic philosophy that was conditioning His people on the earth to abandon Kingdom expansion by focusing on the issues of "making a name for themselves," "Not being scattered," and "going up to heaven." By definition philosophy is "a set of ideas or beliefs relating to a particular field or activity;" so philosophy is a way of thinking. Through Nimrod's leadership the devil was infecting the masses with a demonic doctrine that included as one of its chief tenets, "the philosophy that says going to heaven is more spiritual than subduing the earth to advance God's Kingdom." Another main tenet of this demonic doctrine was "let us build our own kingdom [city or ministry] so that we can make a name for ourselves." Many businesses and ministries today who wear the name of Christ have this motive—some covertly and others overtly. The final tenet of this demonic triad whose three-fold cord would not easily be broken or unraveled was "let us not be scattered." Another way of saying this is, "Let us not be connected with others except our own kind." "Let us not cross pollinate." "Let us be local instead of global." Or "let us be a silo instead of a Shiloh." We will now deal with each of these in turn.

GOD IS INTERCEPTING RAPTURE FEVER

Nimrod's demonic philosophy that says "going to heaven is more spiritual than subduing the earth to advance God's Kingdom" has infected the Church's consciousness masquerading itself as end-time prophecy. God told me that the Church's obsession with the idea of going to heaven is demonically engineered because it causes His people to despise the earth which is our God-given spiritual inheritance. Heaven was never designed for human beings; it was designed for God and His holy angels. This is why angels were created as spirit beings instead of physical beings. Please listen to what the great King David has to say on this important matter.

> *Heaven was never designed for human beings; it was designed for God and His holy angels.*

*Who laid the foundations of the **earth** (emphasis added), that it should not be removed for ever. Psalm 104:5 KJV*

*The heaven, even the **heavens** (emphasis added), are the LORD's: but the earth hath he given to the children of men. Psalm 104:16 KJV*

King David, speaking under the unction of the Holy Spirit, makes it adamantly clear that God laid the foundations of the earth as a permanent habitation for mankind. David says that the earth will never be removed. But it is Psalm 104:16 that completely intercepted and healed me of my "rapture fever." This religious bug had infected me for a very long time. I was born again in a Pentecostal Church were I got more than my fair share of the "Jesus is coming back soon messages." My pastor at the time made it very clear that it was a sheer waste of time to plan too many years into the future, when Christ could return at any second. With messages like this, it is no wonder our church had very few men and women with business acumen. Who could plan for business success if such a plan meant planning ten years ahead? Our favorite church song was "I will fly away!" All my colleagues in the church had a driving obsession to go to heaven. They could not wait to leave this God forsaken planet so they could live in heaven where they will be floating on clouds of glory.

This is why I have a difficult time watching much of what we call Christian TV. Most Christian channels are run by many self-appointed prophecy teachers, who have zero revelation on the gospel of the Kingdom. Many of these prophecy teachers interpret world events from a defeatist and escapist worldview that infects the faithful in the Church with the "religious bug" that causes rapture fever. Some Kingdom citizens never recover from rapture fever till the day they die. It is quite regrettable to say the least.

Do not misconstrue what I am saying to mean that I do not believe in the second coming of Jesus Christ and the advent of His millennial Kingdom here on earth. Nothing could be further from the truth. I believe in the Rapture of the Church in whatever form God has designated for this prophetic event. But the more I study New Testament Scriptures the more I am convinced that the early Church did not suffer from the paralyzing effects of rapture fever. They were obsessed with the idea of turning the world upside down with the gospel of the Kingdom rather than with the idea of going to heaven.

Y2K: WHAT HAPPENED TO THE BUG?

In the transition between the year 1999 and the year 2000 I became completely convinced of the diabolical nature of rapture fever. The fear mongering that I saw on Christian television during the transition to the year 2000 was embarrassing to say the least. There was a rumor that there would be a catastrophic computer crash around the world when the year 2000 came around. Self-appointed computer experts predicted a computer crash because they thought that all computer systems would be unable to recognize the number 2000 in their internal mathematic programming. This, they said, would lead to a catastrophic failure in the communication systems of the world's systems of commerce.

As soon as this unsubstantiated rumor reached the ears of the so-called end-time prophecy teachers, the most embarrassing fear mongering among people of faith started. "This is the end of the world, like we have been telling you in our end-time prophecy seminars," the self- appointed end-time prophecy prophets declared. What baffled me more than the foolishness that these men and women were purporting as God's Word is that many of these end-time prophecy teachers rushed to their publishers to publish their prophetic books about the Y2K bug.

Some self-appointed end-time prophecy prophets had book covers that said "Y2K: the end of the world as we know it!" Even more amazing was the gullibility of their faithful followers who bought thousands of copies of their books on the Y2K bug. I may have been born at night, but I am no one's fool. I am a very contemplative thinker. In my contemplation of the foolishness that I was observing in His church, I asked myself this one question: "If the Y2K bug signified the end of the world, where in the world were these prophetic teachers going to spend all the money that they were collecting from their followers?" I do not know why none of their followers asked them this simple question.

> *Some self appointed end-time prophecy prophets had book covers that said "Y2K: the end of the world as we know it!"*

I know of a mega pastor in Chicago who got his church into a demonic frenzy over the Y2K bug to such an extent that his members started stockpiling gallons of gas and food in their basements. This man told his gullible followers that the Y2K bug was going to wipe out the world's cash system, so they had to buy gold coins from him. His members gave him thousands of dollars in exchange for his gold coins. Once again it would seem like one simple question from a common sense thinker would have placed a stop to the madness. Why did their pastor need their hard currency if cash would be worthless within a couple of weeks? It was then that I became convinced that the Church's obsession with the idea of going to heaven is definitely demonically engineered because it breeds itself into a lopsided view of the world that God called us to transform with the gospel of the Kingdom.

OCCUPY TILL I COME

He said therefore, A certain nobleman went into a far country to receive for himself a kingdom, and to return. [13] And he called his ten servants, and delivered them ten pounds, and said unto them, Occupy till I come. Luke 19:12-14 KJV

Jesus used a parable to help us understand a proper worldview that facilitates the advancement of the Kingdom. Speaking of himself, Jesus said that a certain nobleman went into a far country to receive for himself a Kingdom, and the nobleman told his servants that he would return. Please remember that in this parable Jesus is the nobleman and the far country is Heaven. But when the nobleman (Jesus) left the earth for the "far country," He left a deposit of His Spirit with his servants (the Church) for the purpose of expanding the nobleman's Kingdom. The nobleman also made it very clear how his servants were to advance or grow his interest in the earth. He told them "occupy till I come."

Notice that in this parable the nobleman (Jesus) never told his servants to worry about how and when he was to return. He simply told them to "occupy till His return." The word "occupy" that Jesus used is a military word that is used often to refer to military action which goes beyond invasion of a territory. When a military invasion turns into an occupation, the invading force becomes known as an "occupying force." It is a word used to describe the colonization of a territory by a superior Kingdom. "Occupation" is the first business of Kingdoms because all Kingdoms grow through the process of subjugation through occupation. Consequently "Occupation" is a lengthy and very deliberate process as opposed to invasion. It is lengthy because it involves the systemic takeover of the infrastructure of the conquered nation or colony until every infrastructure in the conquered territory animates the will of the occupying force. The Church can NEVER become an EFFECTIVE OCCUPYING FORCE if it continues to suffer from "rapture fever." If Jesus was to say the same thing in today's language He would say to us "do business or subdue the seven mountains of culture till I come." Jesus would never tell us to worry about our trip to Heaven or when he was going to return. This is why God wants to intercept the Tower of Babel in His church to STOP His people from worrying about matters beyond their control.

THE MOST IMPORTANT BUSINESS ON EARTH

And he said unto them, How is it that ye sought me? wist ye not *that I must be about my Father's **business** (emphasis added)? Luke 2:49 KJV*

Jesus said that we were to "occupy till His return" and the phrase "occupy till I come" also translates "do business till I come." But what business was Jesus referring to? According to Luke 2:49, the business that Jesus wants us to be doing until He returns is the business of advancing His Father's Kingdom. Advancing the Kingdom of God is the number one business of all of creation. Since the Kingdom of God governs all of Heaven there is no way we can advance the Kingdom of God in that realm of eternity, but we can advance God's Kingdom in the earth realm. If we are on earth we can be involved in the business of advancing the Kingdom of God in the earth realm because there are still areas of human activity that are not yet under the government of God. If this is the case, then staying on earth as long as is divinely possible gives us the greatest chance to advance the Kingdom of God. If this is true then rapture fever or the obsession with going to Heaven is definitely the Tower of Babel in His church.

THE GOSPEL OF THE KINGDOM

*And this **gospel** (emphasis added) of the kingdom shall be preached in all the world for a witness unto all nations; and then shall the end come. Matthew 24:14 KJV*

In my opinion what Jesus Christ said in Matthew 24:14 places the icing on the cake and gives us the final antidote against the religious bug called "rapture fever." Jesus told His apprentice apostles that the "gospel of the Kingdom" shall be preached (proclaimed) in the entire world as a witness to all nations, before His second coming. Notice that this passage of Scripture is talking about a phenomenon that many of us have never seen. It is not talking about individuals accepting Christ as Savior, even though this is very important. It is talking about entire nations and people groups becoming acquainted with the gospel of the Kingdom. This is mind boggling to me!

> *Advancing the Kingdom of God is the number one business of all of creation.*

Many people in the Church, not to mention the world, have never heard the gospel of the Kingdom. What many people in the Church have heard is spiritual self help messages under titles such as, *God will see you through, The God of Your Breakthrough, Seven Steps to a Better You.* If you for one moment think that messages such as these are the gospel of the Kingdom then you are in for a rude awakening. The Gospel of the Kingdom is centered on God and His Kingdom. *The Gospel of the Kingdom is not about you; it's about divine occupation of every enterprise of human endeavor, until the Kingdoms of this world become the Kingdoms of God and His Christ* (Rev. 11:15). This is why God is determined to intercept and bring down the Tower of Babel in His Church.

In regards to the second tenet of this demonic triad from the Tower of Babel, God has not called us as his co-laborers, co-creators and co-heirs to make a name for ourselves, but to be ambassadors of the name above all names, the only name by which men can be saved, at which every knee will bow and every tongue confess that Jesus is Lord. He has called us to build according to the heavenly blueprint and the Kingdom pattern, and that involves and includes creating an organizational structure and culture and mission based on Kingdom principles, values, purposes, strategies and technologies. It means we are to be promoters of Jesus and His Kingdom rather than ourselves and our kingdoms, and to walk in humility as well as authority. It means that our true value and worth and ultimate usefulness to God is not based on what men say about us, or even what we say about ourselves, or how big our buildings, campuses, staffs, budgets, attendance and media ministries are, but on what God says about us.

The final tenet of this demonic triad whose three-fold cord would not easily be broken or unraveled except by divine interception from the Godhead was "let us not be scattered." Another way of saying this is, "Let us not be connected with others except our own kind." "Let us not cross pollinate." "Let us be local instead of global." Or "let us be a silo instead of a Shiloh." The first century church had a similar issue and God intervened to accomplish His purposes. "On that day a great persecution broke out against the church at Jerusealem, and all except the apostles were scattered throughout Judea and Samaria" (Acts 8:1). The Great Commission begins with "go ye" or "as you go." God envisions a church of mobile marketplace missionaries, leveraging their gifts and influence to expand the Kingdom into not only unreached people groups but unreached industries, occupations, professions and sectors. Part of our commission is to make disciples of all nations. One of the most effective ways to do that is through the Internet and social media.

As Founder, Chairman & CEO of Kingdom Marketplace Coalition (www.mykmcportal.com), I invite you to visit our website, see what God is doing in the marketplace, and join the movement of God to make disciples of all nations through the marketplace. Cooperation, collaboration, covenant and completion are the new watchwords for Kingdom businesses and entrepreneurs, and God is removing the competitive spirit and the slave mentality and "sweat of our brow" attitude, and breaking the orphan spirit. God is calling His sons and daughters to rise up and come together "as one" to become the army of God and to leverage our resources and influence in the earth.

LIFE APPLICATION SECTION

MEMORY VERSE

At one time all the people of the world spoke the same language and used the same words. [2] As the people migrated to the east, they found a plain in the land of Babylonia and settled there. [3] They began saying to each other, "Let's make bricks and harden them with fire." (In this region bricks were used instead of stone, and tar was used for mortar.) [4] Then they said, "Come, let's build a great city for ourselves with a tower that reaches into the sky. This will make us famous and keep us from being scattered all over the world." Genesis 11:1-4

REFLECTIONS

Who was Nimrod and what did he do?

_____

_____

_____

_____

_____

_____

How has the doctrine of the Tower of Babel affected the Church?

_____

_____

_____

_____

_____

_____

JOURNAL YOUR THOUGHTS

BOOKING

To schedule Dr. Francis Myles to come and speak to your church or business please email us at drmyles@hotmail.com or kmcevents@gmail.com.

Do you need a speaker?

Do you want Dr. Francis Myles to speak to your group or event? Then contact Dr. Bruce Cook at: **(512) 845-3070** or email: **wbcook@att.net** or use the contact form at: **www.kingdomhousepublishing.com**.

Whether you want to purchase bulk copies of *The Spirit of Divine Interception* or buy another book for a friend, get it now at: **www.kingdomhousebooks.net**.

If you have a book that you would like to publish, contact Dr. Bruce Cook, Kingdom House Publishing, (512) 259-8240 or email: info@kingdomhousepublishing.com or use the contact form at: www.kingdomhousepublishing.com.

Made in the USA
Middletown, DE
06 September 2024

60431644R00141